Better Homes and Gardens®

celebrate the
SEASON®
2013

contents

fall

trims

food

gifts

118 SHARE YOUR TALENTS with gifts you've created. You'll find a chapter full of crafts for everyone on your gift list as well as recipes for irresistible sweet treats. The dessert gifts are accompanied by extra-special homemade wraps that make the presentation as wonderful as the treats themselves.

kids

138 GET READY FOR FUN by encouraging the kids to take part in holiday crafting, decorating, and gift giving. Easy painting and paper-crafting techniques are sure to spark young imaginations. These projects are so much fun to make and so professionally polished, the whole family may want to jump in and get crafty.

in a twinkling

EASY TO MAKE, these seasonal sensations are quick to put together and will be much appreciated by all your holiday visitors.

Better Homes and Gardens.

MEREDITH CONSUMER MARKETING
Vice President, Consumer Marketing: Janet Donnelly
Consumer Marketing Product Director: Heather Sorensen
Consumer Marketing Product Manager: Mary Ripperger
Business Manager: Ron Clingman
Associate Director, Production: Al Rodruck

WATERBURY PUBLICATIONS, INC.
Contributing Editors: Sue Banker, Lois White
Contributing Art Director: Cathy Brett
Editorial Director: Lisa Kingsley
Associate Editor: Tricia Bergman
Creative Director: Ken Carlson
Associate Design Director: Doug Samuelson
Contributing Copy Editor: Terri Fredrickson
Contributing Proofreader: Gretchen Kauffman

BETTER HOMES AND GARDENS. MAGAZINE
Editor in Chief: Gayle Goodson Butler
Art Director: Michael D. Belknap
Deputy Editor, Food and Entertaining: Nancy Wall Hopkins
Editorial Assistant: Renee Irey

MEREDITH NATIONAL MEDIA GROUP
President: Tom Harty

MEREDITH CORPORATION
Chairman and Chief Executive Officer: Stephen M. Lacy

In Memoriam: E.T. Meredith III (1933–2003)

the best

When I reflect upon my very best holidays, the most unforgettable Christmases are those spent with family and friends who glowed with holiday spirit and exchanged gifts of true meaning.

Celebrate the Season helps set the groundwork for the merriest of gatherings. With incredible make-it-yourself decorations, extra-special holiday recipes, and fabulous gift-giving ideas, you'll be all set to create unforgettable Christmases of your own.

Set a festive mood with clever table settings that will awe guests. Craft unique tree trims and room accents no store can offer. Whip up irresistible recipes everyone will love—from drinks and appetizers to main courses, sides, and spectacular desserts.

And what's Christmas without gifts? *Celebrate the Season* helps you create handmade treasures sure to bring the biggest smiles from those gathered around the tree.

With hundreds of sparkling ideas awaiting to boost your holiday spirit and creativity, you're sure to make the season a whole lot brighter for those you love.

Wishing you the best holiday season imaginable!

Sue Banker

fall

Give thanks for this glorious time of year with decorations that enhance its beauty.

Bountiful Baskets

Woven baskets are the perfect landing place for autumn-kissed collections.

Planted

Small potted plants work magic in a large basket. To protect the basket and the surface underneath, find a plastic liner that fits the basket and insert it into the bottom. Arrange small potted plants in the liner, leaving space for a short vase or jar filled with a fresh bouquet of fall flowers and berry stems.

Lined

A pretty linen towel or napkin serves as a cushion for a bounty of ready-to-eat fruit. This display is so naturally appealing, it could do double duty as a Thanksgiving centerpiece.

Beribboned

Soften a basket edge with gently curled wire-edged ribbons.
Choose two coordinating ribbons in different widths for
interest, cutting some ends short and allowing others to
wrap around the bottom of the basket.

Tiered

This fun arrangement bursts with color and texture. Choose a round basket and two contrasting wheats. To create the tiered effect, use a wide clear vase that fits into the basket with about 1 inch to spare. Cut enough wheat stems to cover the vase, trimming them 1 inch taller than the vase as shown in Photo A. Attach the stems to the vase using rubber bands as shown in Photo B. To arrange the wheat inside the vase, use a plastic foam ball that fits it snuggly. Trim a slice off the bottom so it sits flat. Arrange wheat, using the foam ball to secure the ends as shown in Photo C; place in vase. Set vase in basket and surround it with short pieces of wheat.

Natural Note

Choose complementary papers to craft a small note card with a horizontal strip near the bottom. Cut out a 1-inch square and layer it on a slightly larger one; glue to stripe. Hot-glue a tiny leaf and acorn to the center of the square. Be sure to have the envelope hand-canceled if it will be delivered by the mail service.

Acorns All Around

They may be small miracles of Mother Nature, but acorns make a big impact on autumn decorating. Before using, wash and dry the acorns, using only those without cracks or holes.

Tied with a Bow

A miniature twig wreath makes an instant napkin ring for any casual dinner. Tie a ribbon bow to the ring and glue a pair of acorns in the center and the napkin ring is a showstopper.

Feathery Friend Look-Alikes

A pair of acorns and snippets of dried leaves combine to make an adorable miniature bird. Hot-glue the pieces together and then to twigs for clever conversation starters. For more feathery friend fun, turn a large acorn cap upside down to act as a nest and place a bitty acorn inside it to resemble a baby bird. Without a cap, the tiny acorn gives the impression that an egg is resting in the nest.

Mark Your Spot

Give a layered paper place card a dimensional boost with acorn and dried leaf accents. A tag board scrapbooking letter personalizes the marker.

The Grandest of Them All

Collect a sack full of similar-size acorns and combine them to make a door decoration to be admired until it's time to hang the Christmas wreath.

WHAT YOU NEED
Tracing paper and
    pencil; scissors
14×18-inch piece of
    ¼-inch plywood
Scrollsaw
Sandpaper; drill
Picture wire
Approximately 150
    acorns in similar sizes
Hot-glue gun and glue
    sticks
Plaid wire-edge ribbon

WHAT YOU DO
1. Trace and enlarge the acorn pattern on page 152. Cut out pattern.
2. On plywood, trace around pattern. Carefully cut out the acorn shape using a scrollsaw. Sand the edges smooth.
3. Drill a pair of holes through wood shape about 1 inch on either side of vertical center and slightly higher than horizontal center. Thread with wire, leaving a short loop on back for hanging; knot wire ends on front; trim tails to ½ inch and hot-glue to wood.
4. Remove caps from washed and dried acorns. Using the photo as a guide, hot-glue rows of caps to the upper portion of the wood cutout.
5. Hot-glue acorn bottoms to the lower portion of the wood cutout.
6. Tie a ribbon bow around stem.

Ring Around the Candle

Squatty votive candles get bumped into designer stature when surrounded with a strip of ribbon and a ring of capless acorns. Choose candles that are contained in a metal, plastic, or glass holder. Trim the edge with ribbon, hot-gluing it in place. Remove caps from acorns and arrange them around the candle. Hot-glue the acorns to the ribbon and to each other.

Full of Thanks

Celebrate Thanksgiving with unexpected metallic accents that make the dining table sparkle.

Come Dine

Create a table that is something to be thankful for in itself. Inexpensive narrow wreaths give the look of natural plate chargers. Using clear glass salad plates allows painted leaves, as well as the dinner plate pattern, to shine through. To add Thanksgiving flair, top each plate with a foil-wrapped chocolate turkey and a pair of pumpkin candies. Trim the table with metallic accents, such as spray-painted pumpkins and dried leaves in a variety of autumn colors.

Gracefully Reserved

Invite guests to find their spot at the table with elegant place cards embellished with a snippet of a metallic gold paper doily.

Autumn-Kissed Favors

Small take-out boxes in rich, falltime metallic colors provide ample room for a handful of candies or small cookies for each guest to take home. Once it's filled, tie each box with a shiny ribbon bow and hot-glue a plastic gem to the center.

Naturally Appealing

Neutral tones blend beautifully with seasonal decorating. Combine logs, pinecones, and birch bark with similar-toned crafts supplies for a calm, nature-kissed palette.

Pretty Posy

A trio of layered buttons makes a pretty floral accent, especially when backed with a pair of leaf shapes cut from birch bark. Hot-glue the layers together and attach to a bowl, vase, or other container using glue dots.

Textural Masterpiece

With a jute-covered plastic foam ring as the base, this button-flower wreath is an attractive accent any time of the year. To hold the jute in place, wrap thick twine around the wreath form, tacking down occasionally with dots of hot glue. Cover the surface with buttons arranged to look like flowers, laying buttons for added detail. Finish with a multi-ply jute bow.

Clever Candle Ring

Birch log slices, drilled like oversized buttons, lace together to make a wonderful geometric centerpiece. Use enough slices to make the ring larger than a pillar candle, filling the space with small pinecones.

WHAT YOU NEED

Birch log slices, approximately
   4 inches in diameter
Paper and scissors
Awl or ice pick
Drill
Gold suede lacing

WHAT YOU DO

1. To guide drill holes, cut a square from paper that fits log slices, allowing ½ inch on all sides. Place it in the center of the log slice as shown in Photo A and mark each corner with an awl.
2. Drill through each log slice where marked as shown in Photo B.
3. Lace the log slices together as shown in Photo C, making Xs on the front side.

Hiking Trail Place Card Holders

Short lengths of birch branches make grand place card stands when topped with pinecones. Cut bark into small banners to use as labels.

Monogrammed Markers

Freehand initials woodburned into log slices serve as place markers, coasters, and paperweights. If the bark slips off the log, hot-glue it in place.

Fall la la la la

Transition your decor
from one season
into the next with
naturals that display
subtle hints of the
holiday ahead.

Greenery-and-Ornament Centerpiece
Trays filled with ornaments make a great
centerpiece. For warmth, temper the shine
with small sprigs of greenery and miniature
pinecones tucked between the ornaments.

Blooming Centerpiece Put a twist on typical fall table decor with a tree-inspired centerpiece. To create the trunk, wrap a clear glass vase with bark chips. At the base, add faux moss and top with nuts, berries, and tiny decorative birds. Add a lush arrangement of hydrangeas, roses, greenery, and hypericum berries.

Peaceful Setting

Wrap Christmas gifts early and put them on display long before the big day. Choose off-white paper to wrap small boxes and top with ribbon that works for both year-end seasons. Hot-glue pinecones around the bow to add a natural touch. Use the package as the focal point for a fall centerpiece.

Casual Elegance

Small earth-tone vases filled with greenery lend a casual vibe. To make the small arrangements sing, tuck in a flower with vivid autumn color along with a berried sprig and small pinecones nestled in the openings. Use these charmers by guests' place settings or align several on a windowsill.

Hydrangea Heaven

Tucked into a landscape of fresh greenery, berries, and pinecones, this hydrangea nosegay lends an unexpected "aha" to an autumn arrangement. Use a low natural-wood bowl to hold the beauties for a grand tribute to Mother Nature.

Cake Stand Display

Show off your homemade holiday treats using cake stands. Stack mismatched stands to create a lovely tiered dessert centerpiece. Keep the decorations as cute as the desserts with mini evergreen plants topped with red stars.

In-A-Twinkling
gourd fun

▲Raised

Replace votive candles and holders with small gourds to bring the colors of the season into a room. Finish the display with a ribbon bow.

Tagged ▶

Scrapbook papers cut into tag shapes look pretty tied to a gourd stem. Use the personalized gourds as place cards or party favors.

Planted

Craft a falltime planter in a jiffy. Remove the stem and carefully cut a circular shape from the center of the gourd, just big enough to fit a flower water tube. Place the tube into the gourd, fill with water and a flower, and tie with raffia in autumn tones.

blessings

fall

Tacked

Paper cutouts and bands make pretty backgrounds to show off seasonal stickers. Attach the trims to gourds using upholstery tacks, gently tapping with a hammer.

Drilled

Long-neck swan gourds work perfectly to hang over a fence or gate. Drill holes into the gourd to hold stems of fresh flowers and foliage. For a longer-lasting bouquet, cut a large hole into the gourd and insert a floral water pick in which to plant the stems.

trims

Let the season begin with jolly Christmas decorations that brighten every room.

Merry Mercury Glass

Reminiscent of the shimmering glass trims of yesteryear, these metallic-coated holders set a festive mood.

Silver and Gold Collaboration

Coat a glass candleholder with silver and gold for a most elegant glow.

WHAT YOU NEED

Glass candleholder
Spray paint in silver and metallic gold
Spray bottle with a 50-50 mixture of vinegar and water
Adhesive gems in crystal and golden tones
Votive candle in a protective plastic or metal holder

WHAT YOU DO

1. In a well-ventilated work area spray-paint the inside of candleholder with a very light coat of silver as shown in Photo A. Immediately spritz the painted area with vinegar water as shown in Photo B, spraying lightly so that the mixture does not run. Let the paint dry.
2. Repeat, using gold spray paint. Mist with vinegar water and let dry.
3. Press gems on one side of the candleholder, making a symmetrical design as desired.
4. Place votive into candleholder. The protective holder will shield against the wax melting onto the paint and pulling it away from the glass.

Jewel-Tone Splash

Throw color into the mix by using metallic spray paints. Check art supply, crafts, and automotive stores for the best selection. Paint the holders as shown in Photos A and B, using colored paint as the top coat.

Singing Praises

Vintage sheet music cut into flag shapes and folded over at the top forms an easy-to-make garland. Tape the edge down on the back and thread the flags onto jute string.

Fun and Frilly

This year, decorate a tree that shines top to bottom with clever touches. The topper is vintage sheet music rolled into different sizes of cones and glued onto a cardboard cone that slips over the tree top.

Striking a Chord

Rolled-up sheet music creates a showstopping wreath. The cone shapes make it easy to fan out the shape, giving it lots of dimension. Hot-glue the cones to a wreath form cut from sturdy cardboard.

Musical Rendition

Cut or rolled, sheet music easily transforms into stunning Christmas decorations.

Vintage Spool Jewel

A wooden spool makes beautiful music as a Christmas tree decoration. Easy to assemble, the trim is a perfect symphony of sheet music, pearl beads, glass glitter, and wire.

WHAT YOU NEED

Ruler
Empty 1¼-inch-tall wooden thread spool
Paper trimmer
Sheet music
Crafts glue
20-gauge crafts wire
Wire cutters
$\frac{7}{16}$- to $1\frac{1}{16}$-inch-diameter mother-of-pearl shank-style button (shank cannot be larger than hole in spool)
Hot-glue gun and glue sticks
Plastic pearl beads: $\frac{7}{16}$- and ¼-inch diameter
Needle-nose pliers
Clear German glass glitter

WHAT YOU DO

1. Measure the height of spool where thread was wrapped. Using a paper trimmer, cut a strip from sheet music to this measurement. Wrap strip around spool. Trim any excess paper. Use crafts glue to adhere end of strip in place.
2. Cut a 6-inch length of wire. Run wire through shank of button, leaving ½ inch on one side of shank. Bend up both wire ends, leaving short end slightly angled to allow for a tight fit when wire is pulled through spool.
3. Feed long end of wire through bottom of spool. Before pushing short wire end into spool, add a bit of hot glue to shank. Push short wire end into spool.
4. Thread large bead, then small bead onto wire at top of spool. Holding beads firmly against spool and referring to the photo, bend wire at a 90-degree angle. Firmly wrap wire around a 1⅛-inch-diameter object (such as the neck of a bottle) to create circular hanger. Curl wire end in a tiny circle using needle-nose pliers.
5. Run a bead of crafts glue along the bottom edge of the spool and sprinkle with glitter. Let dry. Repeat to add glitter to the top edge.

Merry Melody Ornament

For an ornament that sings, fill a clear bauble with bars from a favorite Christmas carol or hymn. Remove the metal topper and gently maneuver strips of music to follow the ornament's curve so the lyrics can be read. Insert five to seven strips, arranging so they line the bowl of the ornament. Shake the ornament a few times so the strips spread out and settle. Keep adding strips in this manner until the ornament is fully lined. Reattach the metal top. Tie onto tree branch with a short length of netting.

Duly Noted

Old sheet music sings a new tune when cut into a spiral and coiled into a rose.

WHAT YOU NEED

Sheet music
Crafts glue
Red seed bead

WHAT YOU DO

1. To make the dainty flower, cut an irregular circle shape from sheet music, about 9 inches in diameter.
2. Referring to the diagram on page 158, cut a spiral into the shape in a continuous coil about ¾ inch wide. The cutting does not need to be perfect.
3. Roll the spiral into a flower shape and glue to secure. Cut a small piece of sheet music slightly smaller than the flower for a base. Glue the bottom of the flower to the base.
4. Glue the red bead to the center of the flower.

Wild Impressions

Make way for a wild approach to holiday decorating.
Mix animal prints with brights for a contemporary look.

Jungle Joy

Bring animal prints to the table with gift boxes, fabrics, ribbons, and simply painted accents. Top each guest's plate with a take-out box filled with sweet treats, tied tightly with ribbon, and topped with a jingle bell.

Striking Stripes

This simple-sew stocking is the ultimate addition to the animal-print decorating theme.

WHAT YOU NEED

Pencil and tracing paper
Scissors
Two 30×18-inch pieces of heavy zebra-print fabric
Two 30×18-inch pieces of bright striped fabric
Sewing machine and matching thread
Sewing needle
Two large tassels in red and white

WHAT YOU DO

1. Trace and enlarge the pattern on page 152; cut out.
2. Use the pattern to cut two pieces from each kind of fabric. Place the zebra-print pieces right sides together; stitch sides using a ½-inch seam. Leave top open. Trim the seams and clip the corners; turn right side out.
3. Place the striped pieces right sides together; stitch using a ½-inch seam. Leave the top open. Trim the seams and clip corners.
4. Slip the striped stocking lining inside the zebra-print stocking. Fold over the top edge of the stocking, approximately ¼ inch. Fold over again, approximately ¾ inch. Topstitch the edge, approximately ⅛ inch from the edge.
5. Fold over a 5½-inch cuff. Stitch the tassels to the upper right corner of the stocking

Place Markers

Fancy place cards use an initial to call guests to their spot at the table. Using small mirror squares, paint black wavy C shapes in a variety of directions; let dry. Paint around the shapes with silver glitter glue. Trim the square with press-on gems and an initial tile. Display on a mini easel.

Zebra Plates

Bring pattern to the table by painting the backs of clear glass plates with zebra-inspired designs (see page 43 for instructions). Edge the black segments with silver and gold to add sparkle.

Gift Wrap in a Snap

Magnified animal prints make a huge impact on holiday wrapping paper. Paint a few oversize designs on wrapping or art paper and let dry. Use glitter glue to accent the designs. Top each package with a ribbon bow and hot-glue jingle bells or a small plastic ornament in the center.

Striking Ornaments

Blanket holiday ornaments with painted leopard print designs that are easier than paint by number. Start by painting black wavy C shapes in a variety of directions as shown in Photo A; let dry. Paint gold glitter blobs inside each of the Cs as shown in Photo B; let dry.

One-of-a-Kind Snowflakes

Embellish pressed-felt snowflakes with easy-to-paint designs. Paint black zebra stripes onto the snowflake as shown in Photo A, allowing space between the marks. Let the paint dry. Outline each of the black designs with silver glitter glue as shown in Photo B. Let the paint dry.

Glitzy Glass

Keep the theme going by dressing up glasses with a zebra-print band. To ensure a straight and even design, place two rubber bands around the glass, keeping straight and parallel. Brush white glass paint between the rubber bands; let dry. Paint black zebra-print designs over the white as shown in Photo A; let dry. Remove the rubber bands. Press lengths of adhesive gems on a roll at each edge of painted design as shown in Photo B.

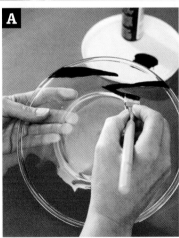

Plate Pizzazz

Give inexpensive dishes a quick makeover with black glass paint and silver and gold glitter glue. Using zebra fabric for inspiration, paint the back side of a clear glass plate with black stripes and V shapes as shown in Photo A. When dry, outline half the shapes in gold as shown in Photo B and the remaining in silver.

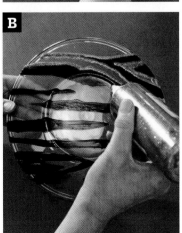

Wrap-Arounds

Small plastic ornaments get a textural covering when wrapped with bakers' string. Use dots of hot glue to hold the string in place. Use the ornaments to embellish candleholders, hang them on the tree, or tie them on wrapped packages.

Candy Cane Touch

Stay in touch with the simple joys of the season with easy-does-it red and white accents brightening your rooms.

Tied Up Tight

Use a strand of bakers' string alongside jute string for a fun tie for a shabby-chic candy container. Wrap a jar with natural burlap, secure with the tie, and fill the jar with candy canes.

Red and White Accents

Enhance a candy cane theme with other items that sing of red and white. Incorporate striped fabrics, chenille stems, white carnations tipped in brilliant red, and ribbon and trims that add to the bold contrast.

Cup o' Candy

Mix and match striped red and white peppermint candies and place them in clear glass mugs for each guest. A tag with a word of joy tied to the base completes the sweet favor.

Chair Bobble

More red than white, this candy cane looks extra special hanging from silver-edged ribbon at the chair's back.

Peppermint Twist

Pep up hot chocolate with flavored marshmallow swizzle sticks. Stir together a cup of sifted powdered sugar with water, 1 teaspoon at a time (3 to 4 teaspoons total), until it is the consistency of a thin glaze. Dip half of each marshmallow in glaze, lightly shaking to remove excess. Roll glazed ends of marshmallows in finely crushed candy canes or peppermint candies. Place on waxed paper, coated side up, to set. Thread on skewers.

Initially Yours

Chenille stems easily twist into any letter of the alphabet. For short pieces, like the A's center line, cut a piece slightly longer than needed and bend over the main part of the letter.

Candle Bright

A piece of jute upholstery webbing cozies up an apothecary jar used as a candleholder. A rustic starfish hot-glued to the front lends a touch of Christmas spirit.

Linen Tricks

Temporarily transform your bed by draping holiday-theme hand towels on the headboard. Red-striped napkins and place mats safety-pinned in place cover the pillows.

Sweet Treat Cone

Stuffed to the brim with decorative shred, this colorful cone makes a grand holder for candy canes or other sweets. Wrap a cardboard cone with holiday-print fabric, cutting to fit and allowing 1 inch to fold over the edge of the cone and the long edges to overlap. Use fabric glue to adhere the fabric to the cone. Fold over the top and glue in place. Use hot glue to cover the seam with pom-pom trim. Hot-glue jumbo rickrack on the inside edge of cone, allowing a scallop edge to show. Hot-glue a ribbon handle to the inside of the cone.

Fun Fabric Trims

Hand-stitched or hot-glued, these colorful projects make a jolly statement wherever they hang.

Happy Scrappy Tree

Bejeweled trees from the 1960s take a twist using contemporary fabric scraps and embroidery. Composed of cut circles, the tree is adorned with buttons, French knots, and straight-stitch stars.

WHAT YOU NEED

Tracing paper and pencil
12×14-inch piece of even-weave white cotton fabric
Water-soluble marking pen
Embroidery floss in green, red, and gold
Embroidery hoop and needle
Coins: half-dollar, quarter, nickel, and dime for patterns
Fabric scraps in assorted red, green, and teal prints; one gold print
½-inch square teal buttons
⅜-inch-diameter red buttons
½-inch-diameter green buttons
Frame with a 7½×9½-inch opening

WHAT YOU DO

1. Enlarge pattern, page 155, onto white paper; do not cut out.
2. Tape pattern to a sunny window or light box. Center white fabric over pattern and tape in place. Trace pattern onto fabric using a water-soluble marking pen.
3. Use three stands of floss for all embroidery. Secure the fabric in an embroidery hoop and embroider words using green stem (outline) stitches.
4. Using coins as pattern templates, draw around coins on assorted fabric scraps. Cut out. Cut a 1-inch square from gold print fabric for a tree trunk.
5. Referring to the photo, fill tree shape with fabric circles, attaching circles with red or green floss and French knots, straight-stitch stars, or with square buttons on top.
6. In spaces between circles sew French knots with green floss and attach red and green buttons with matching floss. Whipstitch tree trunk in place with gold floss.
7. Frame the finished piece.

Shades of Blue

Center of Attention

Set a chunky pillar candle in the middle of a serving tray and place a hurricane over it. Surround the glass with a bed of evergreens, such as berried juniper, and top it with glass ornaments and pinecones for a textural treat.

Silver Bells

Create the look of a miniature tree with lengths of boxwood clippings arranged in mirror glass containers. The luster of silvery out-of-the-ordinary vessels, such as miniature flower vases and bowls, makes tiny evergreens stand out. Provide needed moisture to extend the life of the boxwood by flattening woody stalks with a hammer before arranging them in a vase. Adorn branches with jingle bells.

Nesting Instincts

A footed glass bowl filled with pinecones, glass ornaments, and boxwood clippings creates a sturdy nest for a winter bird at rest.

Draw inspiration from outdoor's winter palette to create a fuss-free display from little more than pretty containers and backyard evergreen clippings.

Window Welcome

Using florist's wire, attach silver pinecones to a purchased wreath. Add a mix of medium and large silver glass ornaments and small tinted ornaments, each tied on with florists's wire. Weave evergreen through the center and to the outside of the wreath for a full, natural look.

Good Tidings

Patterned and solid wrapping paper in silver and blue adds an elegance to even the most humble gifts. Embellish with ribbons, jingle bells, and natural touches.

Simple Settings

Everyday white dishes look fresh and elegant on the holiday table. A colored linen napkin dresses each place setting. Create an attention-grabbing centerpiece with clear glass bottles. Boxwood clippings offer a natural counterpoint to all the sparkle.

Cup of Sweet

Transform your glassware into stylish silverware holders. Trim with a snippet of greenery, a ribbon, and a simple tag.

Darling Details

Little touches contribute to a sweet holiday scheme. Tie a trio of jingle bells together with a length of organza ribbon. Attach to a pillow with a safety pin.

Good Spirits

Fill a serving tray with your favorite sparkling drink and offer guests a glass as they mingle. They'll be sure to hear you coming with glasses adorned with jingle bells.

Perched like bottle corks, silver pinecones top candleholders for an unexpected display. Sprigs of fresh greenery separate the elements.

Jingle Bell Rock

A galvanized pail makes a simple, timeless stand for a white feather tree, which sparkles with dozens of silver jingle bells.

Pillow Perfect

You choose the word or image stencil you like, and these easy-to-make holiday pillows come together with ease.

·I·BRING· ·YOV· GLAD· ·TIDINGS

Rest Your Head

This custom-designed linen pillow bears a merry message applied using stencils and fabric paints. Print the desired message to fit a premade pillow, full size, on a printer. Trace the letters onto adhesive stencil paper for fabric and cut out the shapes using a crafts knife. Adhere the stencil to the pillow. Using a stencil brush, dab fabric paint evenly into the open spaces of the stencil. Following the manufacturer's directions, remove stencil paper.

Have a Seat

Cozy up a chair or sofa with an easy-to-make holiday pillow. Search online for a holiday clip-art image, print it onto transfer paper, and iron it onto fabric to make the panel. Hand-stitch the design onto a purchased pillow using matching thread.

Scholarly Take

Whether ironed on or tacked in place with tiny stitches, this pillow expresses a holiday message in easy-to-read fabric letters available in fabric stores. You can choose whatever seasonal message fits your decor.

Santa's Favorite

Here's the perfect home accent for those who believe in the jolly ol' elf. With a premade pillow cover as the base, use large letter stencils and white fabric paint to add "BELIEVE" across the pillowcase width. To outline with ribbon, use iron-on bonding, following the manufacturer's directions.

Reindeer Play

A felt pillow gets a holiday face-lift with easy-to-cut felt designs. Use the pattern on page 152 or find your own. Cut the shapes from felt and use spray-on adhesive for fabric to adhere the playful duo to the pillow front.

Bringing Out the Brass

Step aside, silver and gold, and make way for classic brass. This metallic tone combines richly with traditional red and green.

Center of Attention

A generous brass ribbon bow spectacularly transforms a plain wreath. Tie a bow with several loops and leave the tails long for big impact.

Dinner Table Touches

From jewelry box to the table, brass brooches add sophistication to place settings. Enclose a fabric napkin with wide satin ribbon. Overlap and secure the ends with a brooch.

Totally Charming

Thick brass wire shapes easily into initial charms to mark glasses at your next holiday gathering. Attach the initials to glass stems by making rings of brass as the connectors.

Door Decor

Mount a brass planter to a door and fill with holiday greenery for a fresh alternative to a wreath.

Eskimo Kisses

Brighten up your holiday scene with an adorable brigade of snowsuited kids frolicking around your Christmas tree.

Playfully Yours

Grab your favorite scrapbook papers and get ready to craft these Eskimo ornaments.

WHAT YOU NEED
Tracing paper and pencil
Scissors
Lightweight white cardboard
Glue stick
Scrapbook papers in assorted prints and black
2-inch-wide wood ovals
Felt in cream and pink
Embroidery floss in black, brown, and red
Sewing needle

Trims, such as chenille stems, pom poms, and ribbon
Fabric glue
Hot-glue gun and glue sticks

WHAT YOU DO
1. Trace the snowsuit pattern on page 154; cut out. Use the pattern to cut shape from lightweight cardboard; cut out. Trace the shoe pattern; cut out. Cut a pair of shoes from black paper for each ornament.
2. Use glue stick to adhere cutout to back side of scrapbook paper; trim around shape.
3. Trace around wood oval onto cream

felt; cut out. Using the diagrams on page 154, stitch eyes and mouth onto felt. Stitch bangs if desired. Use fabric glue to adhere stitched felt to wood oval. Cut out two small circles from pink felt; glue onto face below eyes for cheeks.
4 Hot-glue face onto hood of snowsuit. Trim around the face with chenille stems, hot-gluing in place.
5. Using the photos for inspiration, hot-glue the shoes and trims to the ornaments.
6. Punch a hole at the top of the ornament to thread through a hanger.

Pail o' Plenty

Easier to fill than fabric stockings, these paint pails turned gift holders are super sturdy and add unexpected fun to the mantel. Wrap pails with a strip of glittered scrapbook paper or craft foam; hot-glue in place. Adorn with layered wood and foam snowflakes.

For more sparkle and shine, accent the snowflakes with big and small jingle bells in coordinating colors. To display the cans before Santa arrives to fill them, place plastic ornaments and artificial snowballs inside for a striking presentation.

Greetings with a Smile

This character is happy to welcome guests inside. Use the patterns on page 153 to cut the hood from both lightweight cardboard and scrapbook paper. From felt, cut a face to fit hood and cheeks using pattern. Stitch bangs and smile using embroidery floss. Sew on 1-inch black buttons for the eyes. Hot-glue accents in place as shown.

Top This

For an extra-special package trim, use the patterns on page 153 to cut the hood and scarf shapes from paper and the face and cheeks from felt. Stitch on the lazy daisy hair, and French-knot eyes and mouth with embroidery floss.

Everlasting Gift Gals

Carry the Eskimo theme under the tree with gift boxes all little girls will love. For the large containers, cover oval cardboard boxes with wrapping or scrapbook paper. Cut a hood shape to cover each top, adding a cream or tan oval paper for the face. Use the patterns on page 153 to cut hair, cheeks, mouth, and eyes. Hot-glue feathery or furlike trim around each face and trims as desired.

Too Pretty to Eat
Give a candy bar a grand presentation by wrapping it with shimmering ribbon and topping with a jingle bell.

No-Melt Markers
Let guests know where they are to be seated by adding their initial in sticker form to the center of a snowflake. Nestle it in a holiday pick or two and guests will want to take home the mini arrangement to display in their own homes.

Everlasting Snowflakes
Dust each guest's place at the table with a few flakes of sparkling snow. Dimensional stickers pressed onto each plastic place mat add a special touch.

Pattern Play
It's easy to bring color and pattern to the table while keeping the budget in line. Choose heavy wrapping paper that matches your North Pole theme to make festive table runners.

Snow Angels

Wood gingerbread men shapes are the secret behind these little darlings. Trace around the wood shapes onto scrapbook paper and cut out. Cut oval faces from cream paper to fit and draw on eyes and mouths with marking pen. Trim the snowsuits with snippets of trims, mini jingle bells and buttons, and pom-poms.

Take-Home Snow Globe

Square plastic ornaments take on the look of an oversize ice cube. Hot-glue metallic beads onto mini bottle brush trees. Remove ornament top, put a drop of hot-glue onto the bottom of the tree, and place it inside the ornament using tweezers. Sprinkle artificial snow into the bottom and replace the topper. Press a glitter-covered plastic foam ball onto the wire hanger, gluing into place.

Super-Quick Centerpiece

A pair of skates, a small wrapped package, and a couple of snowball ornaments combine for a festive centerpiece. Add glittered snowflakes, oversize candy canes, and ribbon laces for unexpected touches.

Festive Felt

Inexpensive and easy to work with, felt trims can be made by the dozens and shared during the season of giving.

Out on a Limb

Flex your tree-trimming skills by dangling colorful ornaments in varying styles on snow-white branches.

Felt 3-D Christmas Ornament

Who says felt decorations have to be flat? Give your Christmas tree extra dimension with this 3-D ornament.

WHAT YOU NEED

Tracing paper and pencil
9×12-inch piece each of wool felt:
   two colors
Quick-setting gel glue
Iron
Freezer paper
String
¼-inch-diameter bead

WHAT YOU DO

1. Trace patterns, page 157 onto tracing paper and cut out.
2. Roll a lightweight scrap of paper, such as a magazine subscription card, into a ¼-inch-diameter cylinder that measures the desired height of ornament and secure with glue. Cover cylinder with a layer of felt and glue in place.
3. Using an iron on medium heat, adhere freezer paper, shiny side down, to each color of felt. Using one of the patterns, trace six shapes onto each color of felt. Cut out shapes. Peel off freezer-paper shapes.
4. Run a bead of quick-setting gel glue along the straight edge of each ornament piece and attach to the felt-covered cylinder, alternating colors, until all pieces are attached. Thread string through a small bead; tie ends in a knot to create a hanging loop. Glue bead inside top of the cylinder.

Teardrop Trim

Repeated teardrop shapes combine for simple, colorful additions to the tree.

WHAT YOU NEED

Pinking shears
Wool felt in three colors
Fabric glue
String

WHAT YOU DO

1. Using pinking shears, cut felt into ½-inch-wide strips in the following lengths: 5, 6, and 8½ inches.
2. Form the 5-inch-long strip into a circle, slightly overlapping the ends; glue to secure. Loop the 6-inch-long strip around the 5-inch circle; glue to secure. Referring to the photo, wrap the last felt strip around the smaller two loops, adding a hanging loop of string between the large loop ends; glue together to secure.

Rosette Ornament

For instant elegance, decorate the Christmas tree with handmade felt rosettes.

WHAT YOU NEED

Scissors
Ruler
Wool felt in desired colors
Fabric glue
String

WHAT YOU DO

1. Cut four 1×9-inch strips of the desired color of felt.
2. Fold short ends of one strip into the center of the strip and glue in place, forming a double-petal loop. Repeat with a second felt strip.
3. Glue double-petal loops together in an X shape. Repeat with remaining two strips.
4. To form the rosette, glue together X shapes, placing loops of one X between loops of the other.
5. Glue a felt embellishment, such as a snowflake or circle, in the center of the rosette.
6. Thread string through one of the felt loops and knot the ends to create a hanging loop.

Felt Poinsettia Christmas Ornament

Festive red and white poinsettias pop against your evergreen Christmas tree.

WHAT YOU NEED

(for one large poinsettia and one small poinsettia)
Tracing paper and pencil
Template plastic or lightweight cardboard
Freezer paper
Wool felt in white, dark red, and red
Fabric glue
Clip clothespins
Hole punch
Removable double-sided tape
Ribbon or string

WHAT YOU DO

1. Trace the patterns, page 156, and cut out.
2. Using an iron on medium heat, press freezer paper, shiny side down, onto felt. Place patterns on the freezer paper; trace large poinsettia and large leaf onto white felt, small poinsettia onto dark red felt, and small leaf onto red felt.
3. Cut out shapes and peel off freezer paper.
4. Dab fabric glue on right side of one corner of a leaf; pinch corners together, holding in place with a clothespin.
5. Repeat for each leaf. Let glue dry; remove clothespins.
6. Apply fabric glue to back of leaf and glue to poinsettia between petals. Repeat with other leaves.
7. Use a hole punch to create five dots from white felt for red flower and five dots from red felt for white flower. Glue dots over the glued seam of each folded petal.
8. Form a loop of ribbon or string to hang ornaments from tree.

Felt Snowflake Cutout Christmas Ornament

This ornament's delicate snowflake pattern mounted on bold backing makes a beautiful addition to any Christmas tree.

WHAT YOU NEED

Wool felt in orange, aqua, and white
Fabric glue
Baker's twine
Pinking shears

WHAT YOU DO

1. Trace patterns, page 157, onto tracing paper and cut out.
2. Cut one circle each from red and aqua felt.
3. Cut the snowflake pattern from the aqua circle, folding the shape in half to make the first series of cuts and then refolding in the opposite direction to make a second set of cuts. Fold the shape in half on the diagonal to make a third set of cuts, and then refold on the opposite diagonal to make a final set of cuts.
4. Glue snowflake cutout onto the red circle.
5. Glue a loop of baker's twine to back of ornament for a hanging loop. Glue ornament to white felt, enclosing ends of hanging loop, and cut around shape using pinking shears.

Tree Cutout

These felt ornaments carry out the red, blue, and green color theme but can be made to coordinate with anyone's decor colors.

WHAT YOU NEED

Tracing paper and pencil
Scissors
Iron
Freezer paper
Wool felt in red, light green, green, brown, and aqua
Pinking shears
Fabric glue
Baker's twine

WHAT YOU DO

1. Trace patterns, page 157, onto tracing paper and cut out. Using an iron on medium heat, adhere freezer paper, shiny side down, to each color of felt.
2. Referring to photo, trace pattern shapes on respective felt colors. Cut out shapes, using pinking shears to cut bottom edge of each tree branch.
3. Peel off freezer paper. Glue tree shapes to red oval. Glue a hanging loop of baker's twine to back.
4. Glue ornament to aqua felt, enclosing ends of hanging loop, and cut around shape using pinking shears.

Foot Loose

Kick off the holidays by hanging stockings adorned with an exuberant mix of stripes, snowflakes, and circles. For the stockings trimmed with snowflakes, use clip art for the snowflake designs or draw your own using the photo as a guide.

Snowflakes Stocking

This pretty snowflake stocking adds a bright and cheery decoration to your Christmas mantel.

WHAT YOU NEED

Tracing paper and pencil
Scissors
Freezer paper
18×24-inch rectangle of white wool felt
Scraps of wool felt in red, light blue, lime, and turquoise blue
Quick-setting gel glue
¾×46-inch strip of turquoise blue wool felt
Pinking shears

WHAT YOU DO

1. Trace the stocking pattern, page 158, onto tracing paper; cut out. Using the stocking pattern, cut a stocking front and back from white felt.
2. Find copyright-free snowflake patterns and print them onto the dull sides of 5×7-inch sheets of freezer paper. Using a dry iron on medium heat, press the freezer paper snowflakes, shiny sides down, on desired colors of felt scraps. Cut out the shapes and carefully peel off freezer paper.
3. Arrange the snowflakes on the stocking front; adhere with quick-setting gel glue. Glue the ¾×46-inch turquoise blue strip to the wrong side of the stocking front, starting and stopping at the top edge and letting strip extend about ⅜ inch beyond stocking edges as trim. Glue the back to the front, leaving open at the top. Cut along the blue trim with pinking shears.
4. Cut a 1×10-inch strip for a hanging loop from white felt and fold in half, gluing the ends on the inside of the stocking back.

Stripes Stocking

Mix and match different felt colors to make this striped stocking.

WHAT YOU NEED

Tracing paper and pencil
Scissors
Freezer paper
18×24-inch rectangle of turquoise blue wool felt
Scraps of wool felt in lime, light blue, black, brown, white, and turquoise blue
¾×46-inch strip of white wool felt
Quick-setting gel glue
Pinking shears

WHAT YOU DO

1. Trace the stocking pattern, page 158, onto tracing paper; cut out. Using the stocking pattern, cut a stocking front and back from turquoise blue felt and a heel and toe from lime felt.
2. Following the snowflake stocking instructions, make two felt snowflakes, cutting one in half. Cut scraps of wool felt into various size strips to fit stocking front, trimming some with pinking shears. Cut two ¾×8-inch strips from brown felt to outline the heel and toe.
3. Adhere the felt strips to the stocking with gel glue, gluing the snowflake shapes on a wide white strip. Glue the heel and toe shapes onto the stocking front, along with the brown trim.
4. Assemble and finish stocking as directed for the Snowflakes Stocking, left.

Circles Felt Stocking

Mimic bright Christmas ornament shapes on your handmade stocking with this fun design.

WHAT YOU NEED

Tracing paper and pencil
Scissors
18×24-inch rectangle of white wool felt
Freezer paper
Scraps of wool felt in red, light blue, lime, black, brown, green, royal blue, and turquoise blue
Pinking shears
Quick-setting gel glue
¾×46-inch strip of turquoise blue wool felt

WHAT YOU DO

1. Trace the stocking pattern, page 158, onto tracing paper; cut out. Using the stocking pattern, cut a stocking front and back from white felt.
2. Prepare the circle and star patterns and cut the felt following the instructions for the snowflake stocking, cutting out some circles with pinking shears. Glue circles and star bursts to the stocking front with gel glue.
3. Assemble and finish stocking directed for the Snowflakes Stocking, left.

Pine Art

Set textural felt pinecones atop each place setting for a dash of woodland whimsy. Slip a place card onto the wired stem so guests know where to sit.

WHAT YOU NEED

Tracing paper and pencil
Lightweight cardboard
Freezer paper
Wool felt in two colors
Wooden skewer
Fabric glue
2½-inch length thin wire
Pinking shears

WHAT YOU DO

1. Trace patterns on page 157; cut out. Trace patterns onto lightweight cardboard; cut out.
2. Trace patterns A–E onto the appropriate felt colors the number of times indicated on the patterns. Make a small hole in the center of shapes A–D using the point of sharp scissors.
3. From either color of felt, cut ten ¼- to ½-inch squares to use as separators between pairs of scales. Make a small hole in the center of each square.
4. Slide scales in two-color pairs over a wooden skewer, with a square separator between pairs as follows: Two A scales, square, two B scales, square, two B scales, square, two C scales, square, two C scales, square, two B scales, square, two B scales, square, two A scales, square, two D scales, square, two D scales, square.
5. Shift each pair to position individual petals between petals of the prior pair. Cut excess skewer with scissors. Glue E half-scale pieces into a small flower. Glue flower to top of pinecone.
6. Cut a ¼×2½-inch strip from one felt color for the stem. Twist and glue strip around the thin wire; set aside. Using pinking shears, cut a 1-inch-diameter circle from the same color of felt used to cover stem. Make a small hole in the center of the circle and stem to bottom of pinecone.

Take One, Please
Nestle take-home surprise bottles in a bowl cushioned with paper shred. Accent the display with a pocket watch case filled with glitter, stickers, and a new year wish.

happy 2014

A Year to Remember

While looking to the upcoming year, celebrate New Year's Eve with a touch of nostalgia.

Beautifully Vintage

Set a yesteryear mood with fitting scrapbook papers pieced together to make an inviting place mat. Tag-board scrapbook embellishments pop from the background when adhered to the corner of the dinner plate. Surprise guests with a fresh flower tucked into each dinner napkin.

Striking Napkin Ring

Though they won't actually strike at midnight, small clock faces are fun focal points at each place setting. Found with scrapbooking trims, the clock face attaches to ball chain with a brad poking through the center.

Take-Home Trinkets

Miniature bottles, available with scrapbooking supplies, can hold written memories of the past year or wishes for the year to come. Write thoughts on papers small enough to roll and fit into the bottles. Wrap each bottle with a short strip of paper held in place by a narrow piece of ribbon.

Monogram Marker

Keep glass owners straight with charms of each guest's first initial. Use a scrapbooking chain fob to hold a few charms, including one with a letter.

Timely Place Card

A square of scrapbook paper, folded in half, makes the base for a quick-to-make name card. Layer with a strip of plain paper for the name and finish with a clock face accent, held in place with a brad.

You Are Invited

Layered papers cut into the shape of a tag (see pattern on page 152) make an interesting shape for party invitations. Before adhering the layers, stamp the top plain paper with antique motifs, writing the party information between the designs. Punch a hole in the narrow end and attach a chain fob with a charm or two dangling from the opposite end.

In-A-Twinkling
very vintage

◄Game Board Gathering

Create a scene on a game board with miniatures. Add a border of metallic rickrack to the back, hot-gluing in place and allowing the scallop edge to show. Make a hedge by cutting into a tiny wired wreath and pulling it to elongate the shape. Hot-glue pieces in place on one corner.

Santa Claus Cups ▼

Vintage holiday mugs make unforgettable gift containers. Line clean mugs with cellophane bags, fill with candy or small gifts, and tie at the top with ribbon threaded through a large jingle bell.

Super-Simple Garland ▶

Die-cut greeting cards get a second life when strung garland style. Many old cards are printed on both sides, but if yours are not, glue to patterned scrapbook paper and cut around the shapes. Punch a hole at the top and thread with twine. Tie cards onto a long length of twine.

Toy Joy

A child's metal shovel becomes the foundation for a very special antique door trim. Wire a length of artificial evergreen with pinecones to the handle, hot-glue a couple cute characters to the cones, and tie a jute twine bow at the top.

Tin Grin

Spice tins add a festive touch to any small space. Easy-does-it touches make the containers extra cute.

Classic Rendition ▲

A Christmas record album cover wrapped in tinsel garland is sure to bring smiles. Place it on an easel for presentation, wiring greenery and a bow at the base.

food

Entice holiday guests with spectacular roasts and sides, fabulous party nibbles and sips, and sweet and showy desserts.

Roasts that Impress

Flavorful rubs and glazes and fresh seasonal ingredients make these worthy of being the centerpiece on a holiday table.

PORK RIB ROAST WITH APPLE-CHERRY STUFFING

Pork Rib Roast with Apple-Cherry Stuffing

Ask the butcher to cut this roast from the rib section of the pork loin.

WHAT YOU NEED

1   9- to 10-pound pork rib roast (10 ribs), bones frenched, if desired
    Kosher salt
    Ground black pepper
¾   cup chicken broth
½   cup dried tart red cherries, snipped
½   cup sliced celery (1 stalk)
⅓   cup chopped onion (1 small)
2   tablespoons butter
4   cups dry sourdough bread cubes*
1   cup chopped apple (1 medium)
1   teaspoon snipped fresh sage or
    ½ teaspoon dried sage, crushed
⅛   teaspoon ground black pepper

WHAT YOU DO

1. Preheat oven to 325°F. Trim fat from roast. Place roast, meaty side up, in a shallow roasting pan. Sprinkle with salt and pepper. Insert an oven-going meat thermometer into center of roast. Thermometer should not touch bones. Roast for 1½ hours. Drain off fat.
2. Meanwhile, in a microwave-safe bowl microwave broth for 1 to 2 minutes or until hot. Add cherries; let stand for 5 minutes. Do not drain. In a skillet cook celery and onion in hot butter until tender. Toss together bread cubes, apple, sage, and ⅛ teaspoon pepper. Add cherry and celery mixtures and toss gently. (For a moister stuffing, add another ¼ cup chicken broth.)
3. Loosely pack stuffing beside the roast. Roast for 30 to 45 minutes more or until a meat thermometer in roast registers 145°F to 155°F. Cover with foil and let stand for 15 minutes. (The temperature of the roast will rise during standing.) Serve stuffing with roast. To serve, slice roast between ribs. Makes 10 servings.
*Test Kitchen Tip: To make bread cubes, preheat oven to 300°F. Spread 4 cups of ½-inch cubes in a 15×10×1-inch baking pan. Bake for 10 to 15 minutes or until dry, stirring twice; cool. (Cubes will continue to dry and crisp as they cool.)

Rosemary-Citrus-Brined Turkey

WHAT YOU NEED

2   lemons
2   oranges
8   cups apple cider

ROSEMARY-CITRUS-BRINED TURKEY

1½ cups packed brown sugar
1   cup kosher salt or ¾ cup table salt
1   cup fresh rosemary sprigs
3   tablespoons whole black peppercorns
5   bay leaves
5   cloves garlic, peeled
1   12- to 14-pound turkey
    Vegetable oil
    Ground black pepper

WHAT YOU DO

1. Finely shred peels from lemons and oranges. Juice lemons and oranges.
2. In a 16-quart stockpot combine lemon juice, orange juice, and shredded peels. Add 12 cups water, apple cider, brown sugar, salt, rosemary, peppercorns, bay leaves, and garlic. Cover and heat over high heat until mixture is steaming, stirring occasionally to dissolve sugar and salt. Remove from heat. Add 12 cups ice; let stand until ice melts and mixture is cool.
3. Remove neck and giblets from turkey; rinse turkey cavity. Place turkey in stockpot with brine. Weight down turkey with several plates. Cover; chill for 8 to 12 hours. Remove turkey from brine, pouring excess brine from cavity; discard brine. Pat turkey dry; rub with oil and sprinkle with pepper.
4. Preheat oven to 325°F. Place turkey, breast side up, on a rack in a shallow roasting pan. Tie drumsticks together and twist wing tips under back. Insert an oven-going meat thermometer into the center of an inside thigh muscle. Cover turkey loosely with foil. Roast for 2½ hours. Remove foil; cut kitchen string between drumsticks so thighs cook evenly. Continue roasting for 30 to 75 minutes or until meat thermometer registers 180°F and juices run clear. Remove turkey from oven. Cover with foil; let stand for 15 to 20 minutes before carving. Transfer to a cutting board; carve. Makes 10 to 12 servings.

CORNISH GAME HENS WITH PORT SAUCE

If desired, garnish with watercress, lemon slices, and blackberries. Makes 4 servings.
Port Sauce In a small saucepan combine ½ cup orange juice; ⅓ cup water; ¼ cup port; ¼ cup blackberry spreadable fruit; 2 tablespoons sherry vinegar; 2 tablespoons minced shallot or onion; 2 teaspoons grated fresh ginger; 2 cloves garlic, minced; 1 bay leaf; ½ teaspoon dried thyme, crushed; ¼ teaspoon instant chicken bouillon granules; and, if desired, ¼ teaspoon cayenne pepper. Bring to boiling; reduce heat. Simmer, uncovered, for 5 to 7 minutes or until reduced to about 1 cup. Strain sauce; return to saucepan. In a small bowl combine 2 tablespoons cold water and 1 tablespoon cornstarch; stir into sauce. Cook and stir over medium heat until thickened and bubbly. Remove and discard bay leaf. If desired, store sauce, covered, in the refrigerator for up to 2 days. Reheat before serving.

Marinated Prime Rib

This special-day meat couldn't be easier. Marinating it the day ahead allows it to take on the best flavor.

WHAT YOU NEED
¾ cup dry red wine
½ cup chopped onion (1 medium)
¼ cup water
¼ cup lemon juice
1 tablespoon Worcestershire sauce
1½ teaspoons snipped fresh rosemary or ½ teaspoon dried rosemary, crushed
½ teaspoon dried marjoram, crushed
¼ teaspoon garlic salt
1 4- to 6-pound beef rib roast

WHAT YOU DO
1. For marinade, in a small bowl stir together wine, onion, the water, lemon juice, Worcestershire sauce, rosemary, marjoram, and garlic salt. Place roast in a resealable plastic bag set in a shallow dish. Pour marinade over meat; seal bag. Marinate in the refrigerator for at least 6 hours or up to 24 hours, turning bag occasionally.
2. Preheat oven to 325°F. Drain meat; discard marinade. Place meat, fat side up, in a large roasting pan. Insert an oven-going meat thermometer into center of roast, making sure thermometer does not touch bone. Roast until desired doneness. Allow 1¾ to 2¼ hours for medium-rare (135°F) or 2¼ to 2¾ hours for medium (150°F). Transfer meat to a cutting board. Cover with foil; let stand for 15 minutes before carving. (Meat temperature after standing should be 145°F for medium-rare or 160°F for medium.) Makes 12 to 16 servings.

Cornish Game Hens with Port Sauce

Perfect for a small but elegant holiday dinner, these game hens are doused in a lively sauce made with ginger and blackberry spreadable fruit. Double the recipe for a larger crowd.

WHAT YOU NEED
2 1.5-pound fresh or frozen Cornish game hens
1 recipe Port Sauce
1 tablespoon olive oil
   Watercress (optional)
   Lemon slices (optional)
   Fresh blackberries (optional)

WHAT YOU DO
1. Thaw hens if frozen. Using kitchen shears, split each hen in half by cutting out the backbone. Lay each hen open; use kitchen shears or a large kitchen knife to cut through the breast bone, cutting just off center. Twist wing tips under backs. Place hens, cut sides down, on a roasting rack in a 13×9×2-inch baking pan. Prepare Port Sauce.
2. Preheat oven to 375°F. Brush hens with olive oil. Roast hens for 55 to 60 minutes or until drumsticks move easily in sockets and juices run clear (internal temperature of 180°F on an instant-read thermometer), brushing with Port Sauce during the last 10 to 15 minutes of roasting.
3. In a small saucepan reheat the remaining Port Sauce until boiling; serve with hens.

MARINATED PRIME RIB

Baked Ham with Sautéed Pears and Apples

Look for small jars of red curry paste at Asian markets or in the Asian section of your supermarket.

WHAT YOU NEED

3   cups water
¾   cup sugar
⅓   cup honey
1   teaspoon red curry paste
3   tablespoons butter
4   medium ripe pears, cored and sliced
1   tablespoon chopped fresh ginger
4   medium red cooking apples, cored and sliced
1   5- to 6-pound cooked ham (rump half)
    Snipped fresh thyme

WHAT YOU DO

1. For glaze, in a large saucepan combine the water, sugar, honey, and curry paste. Bring to boiling; stir constantly. Boil gently, uncovered, for 25 to 30 minutes or until slightly thickened; stir occasionally. Cool.
2. In a large skillet melt butter over medium-high heat. Add pears and ginger. Cook for 5 to 7 minutes or until pears begin to brown, gently stirring occasionally. Remove from skillet; keep warm. Add apples to skillet; cook for 5 to 7 minutes or until apples begin to brown, stirring occasionally. Combine apples and pears. Cool.
3. Preheat oven to 325°F. In a large saucepan reheat glaze just until bubbly. Remove ½ cup of the glaze; set remaining glaze aside. Place ham on the rack of a roasting pan. Insert an oven-going meat thermometer into center of ham. Roast for 1½ to 2¼ hours or until thermometer registers 140°F. Brush ham with reserved glaze during the last 20 minutes of roasting.
4. Just before serving, in a large skillet cook and stir fruit over medium heat just until heated through. To serve, arrange fruit on serving platter. Slice ham and arrange on platter with fruit. Drizzle ham and fruit with the remaining glaze. If desired, garnish with thyme sprigs. Makes 16 servings.

Turkey Breast Stuffed with Sausage, Fennel, and Figs

Add bite to the filling by using spicy Italian sausage instead of the sweet version.

WHAT YOU NEED

1   2- to 3-pound boneless turkey breast with skin*
½   teaspoon salt

TURKEY BREAST STUFFED WITH SAUSAGE, FENNEL, AND FIGS

½   teaspoon ground black pepper
8   ounces sweet Italian sausage (casings removed if present)
½   cup thinly sliced green onions (4)
⅓   cup snipped dried figs
¾   teaspoon fennel seeds
¼   teaspoon salt
¼   teaspoon ground black pepper
1   tablespoon olive oil

WHAT YOU DO

1. Place turkey, skin side down, between two pieces of plastic wrap. Using the flat side of a meat mallet, pound lightly from the center to the edges into a square of even thickness. Remove plastic wrap. Sprinkle turkey evenly with the ½ teaspoon salt and the ½ teaspoon pepper.
2. For stuffing, in a medium skillet cook sausage until browned, using a wooden spoon to break up meat as it cooks. Drain off fat. In a medium bowl combine sausage, green onions, figs, and fennel seeds.

3. Spoon stuffing onto turkey. Roll up turkey and stuffing into a spiral. Tie at 2-inch intervals with 100-percent-cotton kitchen string. Sprinkle with the ¼ teaspoon salt and the ¼ teaspoon pepper.
4. Preheat oven to 325°F. Place turkey in a shallow roasting pan. Rub skin with the oil. Roast for 1¼ to 1¾ hours or until turkey is no longer pink (170°F) and an instant-read thermometer inserted into center of the stuffing registers 165°F.
5. Transfer turkey to a cutting board. Cover with foil; let stand for 10 minutes. Remove and discard string before slicing. Makes 8 servings.

*Test Kitchen Tip: If you can't find boneless turkey breast with the skin on, purchase a 4- to 5-pound bone-in turkey breast and remove the bone (or ask your butcher to remove it for you).

Party Pizzazz

These tasty morsels create a cheerful, inviting atmosphere at holiday parties—all make-aheads for your convenience.

MINI GRUYÈRE PUFFS

Mini Gruyère Puffs

WHAT YOU NEED

½   cup water
¼   cup butter
½   teaspoon dried basil, crushed
¼   teaspoon garlic salt
     Dash cayenne pepper
½   cup all-purpose flour
2   eggs
½   cup shredded Gruyère cheese or Swiss
     cheese (2 ounces)
2   tablespoons grated Parmesan cheese
     Grated Gruyère cheese or Swiss
     cheese

WHAT YOU DO

1. Preheat oven to 450°F. Grease a baking sheet; set aside. In a small saucepan combine the water, butter, basil, garlic salt, and cayenne pepper. Bring to boiling over medium heat, stirring to melt butter. Immediately add flour all at once, stirring vigorously. Cook and stir until mixture forms a ball that doesn't separate. Remove from heat. Cool for 5 minutes.

2. Add eggs, one at a time, to mixture in saucepan, beating with a spoon after each addition until smooth. Stir in shredded Gruyère cheese. Drop dough by rounded teaspoons about 2 inches apart onto the prepared baking sheet. Sprinkle with Parmesan cheese.

3. Bake for 10 minutes. Reduce oven temperature to 375°F. Bake for 10 to 12 minutes more or until puffed and golden. Turn off oven. Let puffs stand in oven for 3 minutes. Sprinkle lightly with grated Gruyère cheese. Transfer puffs to a wire rack; serve warm. Makes about 20 puffs.

To Make Ahead: Place puffs in an airtight container; cover. Freeze for up to 1 month. Thaw overnight in the refrigerator. Preheat oven to 325°F. Arrange puffs on a baking sheet. Bake for 10 to 15 minutes or until heated through.

Oregano-Manchego Cheese Straws

Manchego cheese, Spain's most famous cheese, is rich and buttery in flavor with a semihard texture. It pairs well with oregano in these lusciously crispy cheese straws.

WHAT YOU NEED

½   cup grated Manchego cheese
     (2 ounces)
½   teaspoon dried oregano, crushed
¼   teaspoon garlic powder
1   sheet frozen puff pastry (½ of a
     17.3-ounce package), thawed
1   egg
1   tablespoon water

OREGANO-MANCHEGO
CHEESE STRAWS

WHAT YOU DO

1. Preheat oven to 400°F. In a small bowl combine cheese, oregano, and garlic powder. Set aside.

2. On a lightly floured surface, roll pastry sheet into a 14×12-inch rectangle. Cut rectangle in half crosswise to form two 12×7-inch rectangles. In a small bowl whisk together egg and the water. Brush both pastry rectangles lightly with egg mixture.

3. Sprinkle cheese mixture over one of the pastry rectangles. Place the other pastry rectangle, brushed side down, on top of the cheese mixture. Using your fingers, firmly press rectangles together, forcing out air pockets and sealing edges. Brush top with egg mixture.

4. Using a pastry wheel or sharp knife, cut pastry crosswise into ½-inch-wide strips. Arrange strips, 1 inch apart, on ungreased baking sheets. Holding both ends of a strip, twist each strip. Bake for 9 to 11 minutes or until golden and crisp. Transfer to a wire rack; serve warm. Makes 24 straws.

To Make Ahead: Arrange cooled straws in a single layer in a freezer container; cover. Freeze for up to 1 month. To serve, preheat oven to 350°F. Place frozen straws on baking sheet in a single layer. Bake for 5 to 10 minutes or until warm.

MARINATED FETA
AND OLIVES

½ cup white or red balsamic vinegar
4 cloves garlic, minced
1 tablespoon snipped fresh thyme
2 teaspoons snipped fresh oregano
½ teaspoon cracked black pepper

WHAT YOU DO

1. In a large glass or stainless-steel bowl combine cheese cubes, Kalamata and green olives, sweet peppers, and onion wedges.
2. In a screw-top jar combine olive oil, vinegar, garlic, thyme, oregano, and pepper. Cover and shake well. Pour over feta and olive mixture; toss gently to coat.
3. Cover and marinate in the refrigerator for 4 to 6 hours. Serve in appetizer serving spoons. Makes 20 servings.
To Make Ahead: Store olive mixture in the refrigerator for up to 2 days.

Marinated Shrimp Scampi

To thaw frozen shrimp, keep them in the refrigerator for 1 to 2 days or, in a pinch, run them under cold water.

WHAT YOU NEED

¼ cup olive oil
¼ cup dry white wine
6 cloves garlic, minced
2 teaspoons finely shredded lemon peel
½ teaspoon salt
½ teaspoon crushed red pepper
2 pounds fresh or frozen extra-jumbo shrimp in shells (32 to 40)
2 tablespoons fresh Italian parsley
  Lemon wedges

WHAT YOU DO

1. For marinade, in a small bowl combine olive oil, wine, garlic, lemon peel, salt, and crushed red pepper.
2. Thaw shrimp, if frozen. Peel and devein shrimp, leaving tails intact if desired. Rinse shrimp; pat dry with paper towels. Place shrimp in a large resealable plastic bag set in a shallow bowl. Pour marinade over shrimp. Seal bag; turn to coat shrimp. Marinate in the refrigerator for 1 hour.
3. Preheat broiler. Remove shrimp from marinade, reserving marinade. Arrange shrimp on the unheated rack of a broiler pan. Broil 4 to 5 inches from heat for 2 minutes. Turn shrimp over and brush with reserved marinade; discard any remaining marinade. Broil for 2 to 4 minutes more or until shrimp are opaque.
4. Mound shrimp on a serving platter; sprinkle with parsley. Serve with lemon wedges. Makes 10 servings.

Give guests something to talk about with savory bites that are as showy as they are fantastic.

Marinated Feta and Olives

This salty Mediterranean-style appetizer features crumbly cubes of feta cheese, olives, and roasted red pepper coated in a robustly flavored olive oil marinade.

WHAT YOU NEED

16 ounces feta cheese, cut into ½-inch cubes
1 cup pitted Kalamata olives
1 cup pitted green olives
½ cup bottled roasted red sweet peppers, cut into strips
1 red onion, cut into thin wedges
½ cup olive oil

MARINATED SHRIMP SCAMPI

Gorgonzola-Thyme Stuffed Olives

Feel free to swap the Gorgonzola cheese for another kind of blue cheese, such as Roquefort, Stilton, or Danish blue.

WHAT YOU NEED

3   ounces Gorgonzola cheese, crumbled
2   ounces cream cheese, softened
2   teaspoons snipped fresh thyme
½   teaspoon ground black pepper
40 pitted whole green olives
    Fresh thyme sprig (optional)

WHAT YOU DO

1. In a medium bowl combine Gorgonzola cheese and cream cheese. Beat with an electric mixer on medium until creamy. Stir in thyme and pepper.

2. Spoon cheese mixture into a pastry bag fitted with a small round tip. Pipe cheese mixture into each olive. If desired, garnish with thyme sprig. Makes 40 olives.

To Make Ahead: Place olives in an airtight container. Cover and chill for up to 24 hours.

Tricolor Tapenade Toasts

Build a bit of intrigue into the tapenade spread by including Kalamata olives, an imported Greek black olive.

WHAT YOU NEED

¼   cup pitted ripe olives, such as
    Kalamata
¼   cup pimiento-stuffed green olives
¼   cup purchased roasted red sweet
    peppers
1   teaspoon snipped fresh oregano
1   teaspoon olive oil
¼   teaspoon ground black pepper
12 French bread slices, toasted, or melba
    toast rounds
6   ounces soft goat cheese (chèvre)
    Fresh oregano sprigs (optional)

WHAT YOU DO

1. For tapenade, in a food processor combine olives, roasted sweet peppers, oregano, olive oil, and black pepper. Cover and process with several on-off turns until coarsely chopped.

2. To serve, spread toasted bread slices with goat cheese; top with the tapenade. Transfer to a serving plate. If desired, garnish with oregano. Makes 12 servings.

To Make Ahead: Prepare tapenade as directed in Step 1. Transfer to an airtight container; cover. Chill for up to 2 days. Toast French bread slices and store in an airtight container at room temperature for up to 2 days.

TRICOLOR TAPENADE TOASTS

Sweets & Sparklers

Ring in the New Year with decadent, dazzling desserts.

BERRY-LICIOUS
CHEESECAKE

Berry-licious Cheesecake

WHAT YOU NEED

40 vanilla wafers
¼ cup sugar
¼ cup butter, melted
2 cups raspberries, blackberries, and/or blueberries
1 tablespoon berry vodka, blackberry brandy, cherry brandy, or orange juice
3 8-ounce package cream cheese, softened
1 cup sugar
1 teaspoon vanilla
¼ cup sour cream
¼ cup berry vodka, blackberry brandy, cherry brandy, or orange juice
2 eggs, lightly beaten
Sour cream (optional)

WHAT YOU DO

1. Preheat oven to 350°F. Wrap a double layer of foil around the bottom and side of an ungreased 9-inch springform pan to form a watertight seal; set aside.
2. In a food processor combine vanilla wafers and the ¼ cup sugar. Cover and process until wafers are crushed. With machine running, quickly add butter through feed tube. Process with on/off pulses just until wafers are finely crushed, scraping down side to evenly moisten crumbs. Press mixture onto the bottom and 2 inches up the side of prepared pan. Bake about 10 minutes or until golden brown. Cool on a wire rack.
3. Place 1 cup of the berries in a clean food processor. Cover; process until smooth. Press berries through a fine-mesh sieve; discard seeds. Stir in 1 tablespoon vodka; set aside.
4. In a large bowl combine cream cheese, the 1 cup sugar, and vanilla. Beat with an electric mixer on medium until combined. Add ¼ cup sour cream and ¼ cup vodka; beat until smooth. Stir in eggs.
5. Pour about half of the filling into crust, spreading evenly. Sprinkle with 1 cup of the berries. Top with the remaining filling, spreading evenly. Drizzle the pureed berries over top of cheesecake in large zigzag designs or swirls.
6. Place foil-wrapped springform pan in a roasting pan. Pour enough hot water into roasting pan to reach halfway up side of springform pan.
7. Bake for 60 to 70 minutes or until a 2-inch area around the outside edge appears set and the center appears nearly set when gently shaken. Remove springform pan from water. Cool in pan on wire rack for 15 minutes. Using a small sharp knife, loosen crust from side of pan. Cool for 30 minutes. Remove foil. Remove side of pan; cool completely (about 1¼ hours).

CRANBERRY AND ORANGE STRUDEL

Cover and chill overnight. Just before serving, top with additional sour cream if desired. Makes 12 servings.

Triple-Citrus Pound Cake

Pictured on pages 90 and 105.

WHAT YOU NEED

½ cup milk
2 teaspoons finely shredded grapefruit peel
2 teaspoons finely shredded lime peel
2 teaspoons finely shredded orange peel
1 tablespoon grapefruit juice
1½ cups sugar
1¼ cups butter, softened
3 eggs
1 teaspoon vanilla
2¼ cups all-purpose flour
¾ teaspoon baking powder
½ teaspoon baking soda
¼ teaspoon salt
2 tablespoons butter, melted
1 to 2 tablespoons orange juice
¾ cup powdered sugar
Finely shredded orange peel (optional)

WHAT YOU DO

1. Preheat oven to 350°F. Grease and flour a 10-inch fluted tube pan; set aside.
2. Combine milk, 2 teaspoons grapefruit peel, the 2 teaspoons lime peel, 2 teaspoons orange peel, and grapefruit juice.
3. In a large bowl combine sugar and the 1¼ cups butter. Beat with an electric mixer on medium until light and fluffy. Add eggs, one at a time, beating well after each addition. Stir in vanilla.
4. Combine flour, baking powder, baking soda, and salt. Alternately add flour mixture and milk mixture to butter mixture, beating just until moistened after each addition.
5. Spread batter into prepared pan. Bake for 40 to 45 minutes or until a toothpick inserted near the center of the cake comes out clean. Cool in pan on a wire rack for 10 minutes. Remove cake from pan; cool completely on wire rack.

6. To serve, in a small bowl combine 2 tablespoons melted butter and 1 tablespoon of the orange juice. Add powdered sugar; beat until smooth. If necessary, add enough of the remaining 1 tablespoon orange juice to make drizzling consistency. Drizzle over cake. If desired, sprinkle with additional grated orange peel. Makes 16 servings.

Cranberry and Orange Strudel

WHAT YOU NEED

1½ cups cranberries
2 cups peeled, cored, and chopped tart apples (about 2 large)
1 cup packed brown sugar
1 tablespoon water
1 teaspoon finely shredded orange peel
½ teaspoon ground cinnamon
1 3-inch sprig fresh rosemary
¼ cup finely chopped pecans
16 sheets frozen phyllo dough (14×9-inch rectangles), thawed
½ cup butter, melted
Powdered sugar (optional)

WHAT YOU DO

1. In a heavy medium saucepan combine cranberries, apples, brown sugar, the water, orange peel, cinnamon, and rosemary. Cook and stir over medium heat about 15 minutes or until liquid is slightly thickened (mixture will get juicy as it cooks). Remove the rosemary; stir in pecans. Cover and chill for 2 hours or until completely cooled.
2. Preheat oven to 425°F. Line a baking sheet with parchment paper; set aside. Place 1 sheet of phyllo dough on a clean work surface. (As you work, keep the remaining phyllo dough covered with plastic wrap to prevent it from drying out.) Lightly brush phyllo sheet with some of the melted butter. Top with another phyllo sheet and brush with butter. Repeat layering, using 8 sheets of phyllo total. Spoon half of the cranberry mixture on top of the stacked sheets, leaving a 1-inch border on the two short sides and one of the long sides and a 2-inch border on the other long side. Fold the short sides in 1 inch over the filling. Roll up the phyllo and filling, starting from the long side with the 1-inch border. Seal seam by pressing together with fingers. Place the strudel, seam side down, on prepared baking sheet. Repeat with remaining phyllo sheets, butter, and filling to make a second strudel. Brush tops and sides of strudels with remaining melted butter.
3. Bake 15 to 18 minutes or until browned. Carefully transfer strudel to a serving plate. Cool for 15 minutes. If desired, sprinkle with powdered sugar. Serve warm or at room temperature. Makes 12 servings.

ESPRESSO TARTS

Red Velvet Cupcakes with Mascarpone Frosting

WHAT YOU NEED
2¼ cups all-purpose flour
1½ cups sugar
¼ cup unsweetened cocoa powder
1 teaspoon baking soda
1 teaspoon salt
1 cup vegetable oil
1 cup buttermilk or sour milk
2 eggs
1 2-ounce bottle (¼ cup) red food coloring
1 teaspoon vinegar
1 teaspoon vanilla
White Chocolate Whipped Cream
Mascarpone Frosting
White chocolate curls (optional)

WHAT YOU DO
1. Preheat oven to 350°F. Line eighteen 2½-inch muffin cups with paper bake cups; set aside.
2. In a large bowl stir together flour, sugar, cocoa powder, baking soda, and salt. Add oil, buttermilk, eggs, food coloring, vinegar, and vanilla. Beat with an electric mixer on low to medium until combined. Spoon batter into the prepared cups, filling each about three-fourths full.
3. Bake for 18 to 20 minutes or until a wooden toothpick inserted near centers comes out clean. Cool in pans on wire racks for 5 minutes. Remove from pans; cool completely on racks.
4. Prepare White Chocolate Whipped Cream. Prepare Mascarpone Frosting. Transfer the whipped cream to a decorating bag fitted with a large round or star tip. Push tip into the top of each cupcake and force some of the whipped cream inside the cupcake.
5. Generously pipe or spread Mascarpone Frosting onto tops of cupcakes. If desired, sprinkle with white chocolate curls. Makes 18 cupcakes.

White Chocolate Whipped Cream: In a small heavy saucepan combine 3 ounces chopped white baking chocolate and ¼ cup whipping cream. Cook and stir over low heat until chocolate is nearly melted. Remove from heat; stir until smooth. Cool for 15 minutes. In a large bowl beat ¾ cup whipping cream with an electric mixer on medium until soft peaks form. Add the cooled white chocolate mixture. Beat just until stiff peaks form.

Mascarpone Frosting: In a large bowl combine ½ cup mascarpone cheese and ¼ cup softened butter. Beat with an electric mixer on medium to high until smooth. Beat in ½ teaspoon vanilla. Gradually add 4 cups powdered sugar, beating well. Beat in 2 to 3 teaspoons milk, 1 teaspoon at a time, to make spreading consistency.

Espresso Tarts

WHAT YOU NEED
Espresso Cookie Dough
5 ounces semisweet chocolate, chopped
2 tablespoons butter
1 egg
⅓ cup packed brown sugar
1 tablespoon coffee liqueur
2 teaspoons vanilla
½ teaspoon ground cinnamon
¼ teaspoon ground nutmeg
¼ teaspoon ground cardamom
Chocolate Ganache
Chocolate-covered coffee beans (optional)

WHAT YOU DO
1. Prepare Espresso Cookie Dough. If necessary, cover and chill dough for 30 to 60 minutes or until easy to handle.
2. Preheat oven to 325°F. Shape dough into 36 (about 1¼-inch) balls. Press balls onto the bottom and up the sides of 36 ungreased 1¾-inch muffin cups.
3. For filling, in saucepan cook and stir chocolate and butter over low heat until melted and smooth. Remove from heat. Stir in egg, brown sugar, liqueur, vanilla, cinnamon, nutmeg, and cardamom. Spoon filling into each pastry-lined cup.
4. Bake for 15 to 20 minutes or until pastry is just firm and filling is puffed and set. Cool in pans for 5 minutes. Remove tarts from pans; cool completely on wire racks. Spoon Chocolate Ganache onto tarts. If desired, garnish with coffee beans. Makes 36 tarts.

Espresso Cookie Dough: In a large bowl combine ¼ cup butter, softened; ¼ cup shortening; and 2 ounces cream cheese, softened. Beat with an electric mixer on medium for 30 seconds. Add 1 cup packed brown sugar; ½ teaspoon each of baking powder, salt, and ground cinnamon; and ¼ teaspoon ground nutmeg. Beat in 1 egg, 1 tablespoon espresso coffee powder, and 2 teaspoons vanilla. Using 2½ cups all-purpose flour, beat in as much flour as you can. Stir in any remaining flour.

Chocolate Ganache: In a small saucepan combine ⅓ cup whipping cream and 1 teaspoon instant espresso coffee powder. Bring to boiling. Remove from heat. Add 3 ounces chopped semisweet chocolate (do not stir). Let stand for 5 minutes. Stir mixture until smooth.

Loyal Companions

A splendid assortment of sides —stuffing, breads, veggies, and salad—provides plenty of delicious options to round out your holiday feast.

CRANBERRY-APPLE
CORN BREAD STUFFING

Cranberry-Apple Corn Bread Stuffing

Corn bread that is a day or two old crumbles more readily than fresh, so bake or purchase the corn bread for this stuffing at least a day before you prepare it.

WHAT YOU NEED

½ cup butter
1½ cups chopped celery with leaves (3 stalks)
1 cup chopped yellow onion (1 large)
6 cups crumbled corn bread or 6 cups corn bread stuffing mix (two 8-ounce packages)
6 cups dry white or wheat bread cubes
2 cups chopped, unpeeled Granny Smith apples (3 medium)
1 cup dried cranberries, dried cherries, or raisins
2 tablespoons snipped fresh sage or 1½ teaspoons dried sage, crushed
1 tablespoon snipped fresh thyme or 1 teaspoon dried thyme, crushed
½ teaspoon salt
½ teaspoon ground black pepper
1¾ to 2 cups chicken broth (if using stuffing mix, use 3 to 3¼ cups broth)

WHAT YOU DO

1. Preheat oven to 325°F. In a large Dutch oven melt butter over medium heat. Add celery and onion; cook and stir about 5 minutes or until tender. Remove from heat. Stir corn bread, bread cubes, apples, cranberries, sage, thyme, salt, and pepper into onion mixture. Drizzle with enough broth to moisten, tossing mixture lightly to combine.
2. Spoon stuffing into a 3-quart rectangular baking dish. Bake, covered, for 35 minutes. Uncover and bake for 15 to 20 minutes more or until hot in center (165°F.) Makes 12 servings.

Dill and Cheese Beer Bread

For the best flavor, be sure to use a light-color beer in this bread. Darker beers may cause it to have a bitter taste.

WHAT YOU NEED

3 cups all-purpose flour
2 tablespoons sugar
1 tablespoon baking powder
1 tablespoon dill seeds
1 teaspoon salt
1 teaspoon dried dillweed
¾ teaspoon baking soda

DILL AND CHEESE BEER BREAD

½ cup shredded cheddar cheese (2 ounces)
½ cup shredded Monterey Jack cheese with jalapeño chile peppers (2 ounces)
1 12-ounce can beer
Garlic Butter or Herb Butter

WHAT YOU DO

1. Preheat oven to 350°F. Grease bottom and ½ inch up sides of a 9×5×3-inch loaf pan; set aside.
2. In a large bowl stir together flour, sugar, baking powder, dill seeds, salt, dried dillweed, and baking soda. Add cheddar cheese and Monterey Jack cheese; toss gently to coat. Slowly add beer, stirring until combined (batter will be very thick). Spoon the batter into the prepared pan, spreading evenly to edges.

3. Bake about 45 minutes or until a toothpick inserted near the center comes out clean. Cool in pan on a wire rack for 10 minutes. Remove bread from pan. Cool completely on wire rack. Serve with Garlic Butter or Herb Butter.
4. Tightly wrap bread. Let stand at room temperature for up to 24 hours before slicing. (Or for longer storage, chill for up to 3 days or freeze for up to 1 month. Let come to room temperature before serving.) Makes 1 loaf or 16 servings.
Garlic Butter: Stir together ½ cup softened butter and 3 cloves minced garlic. Cover and chill for up to 1 week. Makes ½ cup.
Herb Butter: Stir together ½ cup softened butter, 1 tablespoon of your favorite fresh herbs, and ½ teaspoon freshly ground black pepper. Cover and chill for up to 1 week. Makes ½ cup.

BACON-TOPPED
GREEN BEAN CASSEROLE

Bacon-Topped Green Bean Casserole

Who would guess that this classic casserole could get even more delicious? Bacon and wild mushrooms make this extra flavorful.

WHAT YOU NEED

1½ pounds fresh green beans, trimmed
1   cup boiling water
½   ounce dried wild mushrooms, such as morel, chantarelle, oyster, and/or porcini mushrooms
7   to 8 slices bacon (8 ounces), cut into small pieces
12   ounces cremini mushrooms, sliced
2   cloves garlic, minced
3   tablespoons butter
3   tablespoons all-purpose flour
2   cups half-and-half or light cream
2   teaspoons snipped fresh rosemary or ½ teaspoon dried rosemary, crushed
1   teaspoon salt
½   teaspoon ground black pepper

WHAT YOU DO

1. In an extra-large skillet cook beans in boiling lightly salted water about 3 minutes or until crisp-tender; drain. Transfer to a bowl of ice water to stop cooking. Drain again; set aside.
2. Meanwhile, in a small bowl pour the 1 cup boiling water over the dried mushrooms. Cover and let stand for 15 minutes.
3. In the same extra-large skillet cook bacon until crisp. Using a slotted spoon, transfer bacon to a small bowl lined with a paper towel; crumble bacon. Reserve about 1 tablespoon of the bacon drippings in skillet; discard the remaining drippings. Cook cremini mushrooms in the reserved drippings over medium-high heat until lightly browned, stirring occasionally. Stir in garlic. Cook and stir for 1 minute more. Remove from heat. Stir in green beans.
4. Meanwhile, use a fork to remove the dried mushrooms from the water (do not discard liquid). Chop the mushrooms; add to green bean mixture.
5. For sauce, in a medium saucepan melt butter over medium heat. Stir in flour. Cook and stir for 1 minute. Stir in all but about 2 tablespoons of the mushroom liquid (discard the liquid at the bottom of the bowl, which may be gritty). Stir in half-and-half. Cook and stir over medium heat until thickened and bubbly. Cook and stir for 1 minute more. Remove from heat. Stir in rosemary, salt, and pepper.
6. Preheat oven to 375°F. Stir the sauce into the bean mixture. Spoon into a 2-quart square baking dish. Bake for 25 to 30 minutes or until bubbly. Top with bacon. Bake for 5 minutes more. Makes 8 servings.
To Make Ahead: Transfer crumbled bacon, green bean mixture, and sauce to separate airtight containers. Cover and chill for up to 24 hours. Continue with Step 6.

Persimmon, Orange, and Pomegranate Salad

Persimmons are widely available in the winter. If you can't find them, mangoes or papayas are delicious replacements.

WHAT YOU NEED

1   pomegranate
2   large ripe Fuyu persimmons,* mangoes, or papayas
5   cups mesclun, arugula, baby arugula, or mixed salad greens
6   tablespoons thinly sliced green onions (3)
     Pine Nut-Persimmon Vinaigrette
4   medium cara cara, blood, and/or navel oranges, peeled and thinly sliced*

WHAT YOU DO

1. Score an "X" into the top of the pomegranate. Break apart into quarters. Working in a bowl of cool water, immerse each quarter; use your fingers to loosen the seeds from the white membrane. Discard the peel and membrane. Drain the seeds; set aside.
2. Cut each persimmon in half; remove core. Slice into ¼- to ½-inch slices.
3. In a large bowl combine mesclun and green onions. Drizzle ½ cup of the Pine Nut-Persimmon Vinaigrette over musclun; toss to coat.
4. To serve, arrange mesclun mixture on six chilled salad plates. Arrange persimmons and oranges on top of greens, tucking a few in and under leaves. Sprinkle with pomegranate seeds. Pass the remaining Pine Nut-Persimmon Vinaigrette. Makes 6 servings.
Pine Nut-Persimmon Vinaigrette: Remove the core from one large ripe Fuyu persimmon;* cut in half. Scoop out pulp (you should have about ⅓ cup), discarding skin. (Or use ⅓ cup mango or papaya pulp.) Place pulp in a blender or food processor. Cover and blend or process until smooth. Add ⅓ cup olive oil; ¼ cup red or white wine vinegar; 3 tablespoons toasted pine nuts; 1½ teaspoons finely shredded orange peel; 2 tablespoons orange juice; 1 tablespoon honey; ½ of a large shallot, cut up; ½ teaspoon Dijon mustard; dash ground cinnamon or ground allspice; and dash freshly ground black pepper. Cover and blend or process until smooth. Makes about 1¼ cups.
*Test Kitchen Tip: Short, squatty, and crisp Fuyu persimmons are the ones to use in this salad. (The acorn-shape Hachiya must ripen to a gelatinous softness to be edible and is usually used for baking.)

CAULIFLOWER-FONTINA GRATIN

Cauliflower-Fontina Gratin

Creamy, buttery, and nutty Fontina cheese—one of Italy's famous cheeses—tastes amazing when it's paired with cauliflower and baked to melty perfection.

WHAT YOU NEED

6   cups cauliflower florets (2 small heads)
¼   cup butter
¼   cup all-purpose flour
2   cups half-and-half, light cream, or milk
½   cup milk
¾   cup shredded Fontina cheese (3 ounces)
1   tablespoon snipped fresh thyme or 1 teaspoon dried thyme, crushed
½   teaspoon salt
¼   teaspoon ground black pepper
⅔   cup soft bread crumbs
2   tablespoons olive oil
     Snipped fresh thyme (optional)

WHAT YOU DO

1. Lightly grease a 2-quart square baking dish; set aside. In a Dutch oven cook cauliflower in boiling lightly salted water about 5 minutes or just until tender; drain. Transfer to a bowl of ice water to stop cooking. Drain again; set aside.
2. In a medium saucepan melt butter over medium-low heat. Stir in flour. Cook and stir for 1 minute. Stir in half-and-half and the ½ cup milk. Cook and stir over medium heat until thickened and bubbly. Cook and stir for 1 minute more. Remove from heat. Stir in Fontina cheese, the 1 tablespoon fresh thyme, the salt, and pepper.
3. Spread about 1 cup of the sauce evenly in the bottom of the prepared dish. Arrange cauliflower florets in an even layer in the baking dish. Spread the remaining sauce over the cauliflower.
4. Preheat oven to 375°F. Let chilled gratin stand at room temperature for 30 minutes before baking. If chilled, remove plastic wrap. Sprinkle gratin evenly with bread crumbs; drizzle evenly with olive oil. Bake for 25 to 30 minutes or until lightly browned and bubbly. If desired, sprinkle with additional snipped fresh thyme. Makes 12 servings.
To Make Ahead: After completing Step 3, cover dish with plastic wrap and chill for up to 24 hours. Continue with Step 4.

CHEDDAR-CORNMEAL ROLLS

Cheddar-Cornmeal Rolls

WHAT YOU NEED

4   to 4½ cups all-purpose flour
¾   cup cornmeal
2   packages active dry yeast
1¼   cups buttermilk or sour milk*
¼   cup sugar
3   tablespoons butter or vegetable oil
3   tablespoons Dijon mustard
1   teaspoon salt
1   cup shredded sharp cheddar cheese (4 ounces)
2   eggs
     Roasted Red Pepper Butter (optional)

WHAT YOU DO

1. In a large bowl combine 1 ½ cups of the flour, the cornmeal, and yeast; set aside. In a small saucepan combine buttermilk, sugar, butter, mustard, and salt. Heat and stir just until warm (120°F to 130°F). Add buttermilk mixture, cheese, and eggs to flour mixture.
2. Beat with an electric mixer on low to medium for 30 seconds, scraping sides of bowl constantly. Beat on high for 3 minutes. Using a wooden spoon, stir in as much of the remaining flour as you can.
3. Turn dough out onto a lightly floured surface. Knead in enough of the remaining flour to make a moderately stiff dough that is smooth and elastic (6 to 8 minutes total).

Shape into a ball. Place dough in a lightly greased large bowl, turning once to grease surface. Cover; let rise in a warm place until double in size (about 1½ hours).
4. Punch dough down; turn out onto a lightly floured surface. Divide dough in half. Cover; let rest for 10 minutes. Lightly grease twenty-four 2½-inch muffin cups.
5. Divide each dough half into 36 portions. Shape each portion into a ball, pulling edges under to make a smooth top. Place three balls, smooth sides up, in each prepared muffin cup. Cover muffin pans. Let rise in a warm place until nearly double in size (about 45 minutes).
6. Preheat oven to 375°F. Bake about 15 minutes or until rolls sound hollow when lightly tapped. Immediately remove from muffin cups; cool slightly on wire racks. Serve warm. If desired, serve with Roasted Red Pepper Butter. Makes 24 servings.
Roasted Red Pepper Butter: Thoroughly drain ¼ cup chopped bottled roasted red sweet peppers; pat dry with paper towels. In a food processor combine the chopped peppers; ½ cup butter, softened and cut up; and 1 clove garlic, minced. Cover and process until well mixed.
***Test Kitchen Tip:** To make 1¼ cups sour milk, place 4 teaspoons lemon juice or vinegar in a glass measuring cup. Add enough milk to make 1¼ cups total liquid; stir. Let stand for 5 minutes before using.

In-a-Twinkling
holiday sips

◄ Sangrias

In a 3-quart glass pitcher stir together 2 cups cranberry juice and 1 cup freshly squeezed clementine juice. Add two 750-milliliter bottles dry red wine and ½ to ⅔ cup sugar, stirring until sugar dissolves. Cover; chill for at least 3 hours. Stir in lemon slices, raspberries, and some ice cubes before serving. Makes 12 (6-ounce) servings.

▼ Pom-Berry Margaritas

Rub a lemon wedge around rims of six margarita glasses. Dip rims into sugar; set aside. In a blender combine ¾ cup pomegranate juice, ½ cup tequila, ⅓ cup raspberry liqueur, and ¼ cup pomegranate liqueur. Cover and blend, adding ice until mixture becomes slushy. Serve immediately in prepared glasses. Makes 6 servings.

Hot Buttered Yum ◄

Fill a spice bag with three 1-inch-long strips lemon peel, 3 inches stick cinnamon, and 1 teaspoon whole cloves. Add bag to a 3½-quart s low cooker with 4 cups cranberry-raspberry juice blend, 2 cups apple cider, 2 c ups water, ½ cup sugar, and ¼ cup lemon juice. Cover; cook on high-heat setting for 3½ to 4 hours. Discard spice bag. Serve in heatproof mugs. Makes 8 servings.

▼Winter Grapefruit Martini

In a cocktail shaker combine ½ cup gin, 2 tablespoons grapefruit juice, 1 tablespoon Simple Syrup,* 1 tablespoon dry vermouth, and 1 teaspoon lemon juice; shake to combine. Add; cover and shake until very cold. Strain into chilled martini glasses. Makes 2 servings.

*Simple Syrup: In a saucepan combine equal parts water and sugar. Cook and stir until sugar is dissolved. Cool; store in the refrigerator.

Pineapple-Ginger Punch ►

In a saucepan combine 1 cup water, ½ cup sugar, and ⅔ cup thinly sliced, unpeeled fresh ginger. Bring to boiling; reduce heat. Simmer, uncovered, for 10 minutes. Cool, strain, and chill. Combine mixture with 2½ cups unsweetened pineapple juice and 3 tablespoons each of lemon and lime juice. Stir in a 1-liter bottle club soda, chilled. Makes 8 (6-ounce) servings.

gifts

Surprises under the tree are unforgettable when you create them yourself and hide them inside glowing wraps.

Taking Off the Chill

Family and friends will love finding these cozy comforts waiting for them under the Christmas tree.

Holly and Berry Throw

Whether you love to felt or are new to the technique, this project will have you creating throws for everyone on your gift list.

WHAT YOU NEED
Tracing paper and pencil
Scissors
Wool felt in olive green and ivory
Afghan
Roving in green, red, orange, and bright pink
Felting needle and brush backing pad

WHAT YOU DO
1. Trace the holly and berry patterns on page 156; cut out. Use the patterns to cut inner holly shapes from olive green and the outer holly shapes and three berries from ivory felt.
2. For each holly leaf, felt a green vein onto each leaf as shown in Photo A following the manufacturer's directions to press the roving into the felt. Trim off excess roving as shown in Photo B. Felt the green holly leaf shape to the ivory background shape as shown in Photo C.
3. For each berry, place ivory felt circle onto brush backing pad. Start by felting the berry in the center using red roving as shown in Photo D. Wind the roving around as you work. Felt an area about the size of a quarter and cut off the excess roving. Secure the red end before moving on to orange and pink as shown in Photo E.
4. With the backing pad in place and working on one felt piece at a time, arrange and felt each piece to one afghan corner as shown in Photo F.

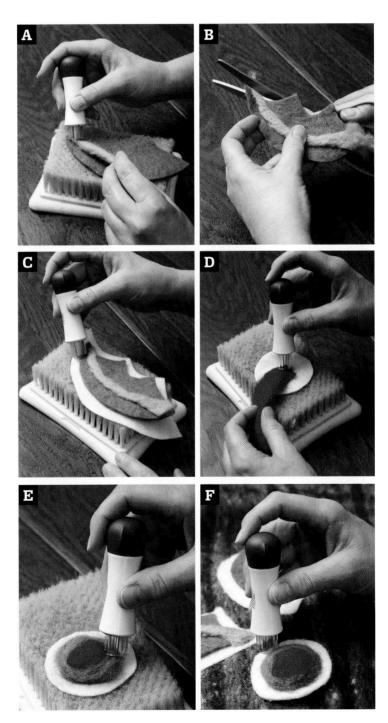

Blooming Border

Plaid wool scarves can't be beat when it comes to keeping warm on wintry days. Make scarves unique by stitching a border that looks high-end but is simple to achieve. Start by stitching a narrow ribbon 2 inches from one scarf end. Use big cross-stitches (see page 156 for diagrams) and embroidery floss to tack ribbon down. Sew buttons on one end, adding ribbon stems and leaves. Running stitches tack stem ribbons in place.

Well Worn

Warm an interior space with a cleverly concocted centerpiece. Scour flea markets and second-hand shops for wintery shoes and boots that would make a nice appearance on the table instead of under it.

Posy Slippers

All the gals on your gift list will want a pair of these hand-embellished slippers. Choose three felt colors for flowers and green for leaves. Use the patterns on page 155 to cut the shapes from felt. Roll the uncut edge of the felt center stamen piece. Fold the felt circle in half and tuck the rolled stamen end into the center of the folded circle; tack in place with embroidery floss. Fold the felt circle in half the other direction and tack again, catching the stamen in the center. Using matching embroidery floss, sew a running stitch down the center of the leaf. Sew layers together as shown in the photo, knotting floss on the back side. Tack to each slipper using embroidery floss or attach with large safety pins from the inside of the slipper.

Mitten Magic

Purchased mittens get a cute upgrade when decked out with ribbon and jingle bell accents. Tie two bows from ⅜-inch ribbon, trimming the ends at an angle. Overlap the bows and hand-stitch to each mitten cuff, tacking a jingle bell in the center.

Craft a ruffled wreath from strips of cotton fabric hand-gathered into ruffles and hot-glued to a plastic foam wreath form. Black and white photos punched with a hole at the top tie onto greenery hot-glued to the ruffles.

Photo Fun

Give family and friends memory-making gifts, using photos that will warm their hearts.

Feathered Nest

Computer-printed photos on textured cardstock bring personality to an already decked-out tree. Trim the tree first, then hang the photos scattered evenly across the tree.

Get Charged

Here's a great way to use all the wonderful photo cards that fill your mailbox during the holiday season. Trace around the edge of a plastic charger onto paper. Mark the rim area and cut it out. Arrange photos on the paper pattern to find the best placement, trimming as needed. Tape the photos together on the back and cut out the donut shape using the pattern. Temporarily adhere the photo border to a charger using double-sided tape. To adhere them permanently, use crafts glue.

Charming Tree Trims

Available with jewelry making supplies, photo charms make adorable mini ornaments. Place photos between the glass pieces and wire on a small charm, bead, or initial— whatever enhances the photo. Tie a ribbon bow to the hanger.

For You

Use a dear one's photo to indicate the gift's recipient. Place their photo in a frame ornament, tying a pair of tassels to the top.

Sweet Giving

From decadent sweets to savory treats, homemade gifts are the best kind, especially when they're prettily packaged.

CRANBERRY-CANDIED GINGER
BLONDIES WITH TOASTED
MACADAMIAS

Cherry-Cashew Milk Chocolate Bark

WHAT YOU NEED

8 ounces chocolate-flavor candy coating, chopped (1 cup)
6 ounces milk chocolate, chopped (1 cup)
1 tablespoon shortening
½ cup cashews, toasted
½ cup snipped dried cherries
2 ounces finely chopped milk chocolate (⅓ cup)

WHAT YOU DO

1. Line a large baking sheet with heavy foil; grease foil and set aside.
2. In a large microwave-safe bowl combine chopped candy coating, 1 cup chopped chocolate, and shortening. Microwave, uncovered, on 100% power (high) for 1½ to 2 minutes or until melted, stirring every 30 seconds.
3. Pour mixture onto prepared baking sheet. Spread to about ¼ inch thick. Sprinkle cashews, dried cherries, and ⅓ cup chopped chocolate over mixture on baking sheet, pressing lightly with the back of a spoon.
4. Chill candy until firm, about 30 minutes. Use foil to lift candy from baking sheet; carefully break candy into pieces. Store candy between layers of waxed paper in an airtight container in the refrigerator for up to 2 weeks.

So Elegant

Bars stack beautifully in wide-mouth teacups. Scour thrift shops for pretty cups and saucers that are matching or coordinating. Place a short stack of bars in a cellophane bag and tie with gold cord. To make an initial gift tag, use a precut snowflake and add a circle of white paper topped with a glittered initial sticker. Hot-glue a metallic gold chenille stem around the circle.

Cranberry-Candied Ginger Blondies with Toasted Macadamias

WHAT YOU NEED

12 ounces white baking chocolate, chopped
½ cup butter, cut up
3 eggs
½ cup sugar
1¾ cups all-purpose flour
1 teaspoon vanilla
1 cup macadamia nuts, coarsely chopped
½ cup dried cranberries, chopped

Prettied-Up Cup

Giving homemade candy in a paper cup is an inexpensive wrap. To dress it up, trim the rim with a evergreen chenille stem, hot-gluing it in place. Tie a generous ribbon bow and adhere it to one side with a mini holiday sprig.

CHERRY-CASHEW MILK

2 tablespoons finely chopped crystallized ginger
4 ounces white baking chocolate (optional)
1 tablespoon shortening (optional)
2 tablespoons finely chopped crystallized ginger (optional)
   Chopped dried cranberries (optional)

WHAT YOU DO

1. Preheat oven to 350°F. Line a 13×9×2-inch baking pan with foil, extending the foil over the edges of the pan. Lightly grease foil; set pan aside.
2. In a medium saucepan heat and stir the 12 ounces white chocolate over low heat until melted and smooth. Remove from heat; stir in butter until melted. Let cool for 15 minutes.
3. Add eggs and sugar to melted chocolate mixture. Whisk until smooth. Stir in flour and vanilla just until smooth. Fold in nuts, cranberries, and 2 tablespoons ginger.
4. Spread the batter evenly in the prepared pan. Bake for 28 to 30 minutes or until top is light brown and sides begin to pull away from pan. Cool in pan on a wire rack.
5. If desired, in a small saucepan heat and stir 4 ounces white chocolate and shortening over low heat until melted and smooth. Drizzle over cooled bars and sprinkle with 2 tablespoons ginger and additional chopped dried cranberries.
6. Use foil to lift uncut bars out of pan to a cutting board. Cut into bars. Makes 32.
To Store: Layer cookies between sheets of waxed paper in an airtight container; cover. Store at room temperature for up to 3 days or freeze for up to 3 months.

Puttin' on the Ritz

Paper plates usually lack pizzazz, but this one has "special" written all over it. From the rickrack edging hot-glued to the underside to the ornament-trimmed corner, this cookie plate makes the meringue cookies even more of a treat.

FRENCH FILLED MACAROONS

French Filled Macaroons

WHAT YOU NEED

1¼ cups powdered sugar
1 cup finely ground almonds
3 egg whites
½ teaspoon vanilla
Dash salt
¼ cup granulated sugar
1 to 2 drops red or green food coloring
Cherry Filling or Chocolate Filling

1. Line three large cookie sheets with parchment paper; set aside. Stir together powdered sugar and nuts; set aside.
2. In a large bowl combine egg whites, vanilla, and salt. Beat with an electric mixer on medium until soft peaks form (tips curl). Gradually add granulated sugar, about 1 tablespoon at a time, beating on high just until stiff peaks form (tips stand straight). Stir in nut mixture and food coloring.
3. Spoon mixture into a large decorating bag fitted with a large (about ½-inch) round tip. Pipe 1½-inch circles 1 inch apart onto the prepared cookie sheets. Let stand for 30 minutes before baking.
4. Preheat oven to 325°F. Bake cookies about 10 minutes or just until set. Cool on cookie sheets on wire racks. Peel cookies off parchment paper.

5. Spread about 1 teaspoon of the Cherry Filling or Chocolate Filling on bottoms of half of the cookies. Top with the remaining cookies, bottom sides down. Makes 32 cookie sandwiches.

Cherry Filling: In a medium bowl beat 3 tablespoons softened butter with an electric mixer on medium to high for 30 seconds. Add 1 cup powdered sugar, 1 tablespoon maraschino cherry juice, and ½ teaspoon vanilla; beat until combined. Beat in 1 cup additional powdered sugar. If necessary, beat in additional maraschino cherry juice (2 to 3 teaspoons) to make filling spreading consistency. Tint bright pink with red food coloring. Makes about 1 cup.

Chocolate Filling: In a medium bowl beat 3 tablespoons softened butter with an electric mixer on medium to high for 30 seconds. Add 1 cup powdered sugar, 2 tablespoons unsweetened cocoa powder, 1 tablespoon milk, and ½ teaspoon vanilla; beat until combined. Beat in 1 cup additional powdered sugar. If necessary, beat in additional milk (2 to 3 teaspoons) to make filling spreading consistency. Makes about 1 cup.

To Store: Layer unfilled cookies between sheets of waxed paper in an airtight container; cover. Store in refrigerator for up to 3 days or freeze for up to 3 months.

Snickerdoodle Snack Mix

WHAT YOU NEED

1 3.5-ounce bag unpopped low-fat butter-flavor microwave popcorn
4½ teaspoons sugar
¼ teaspoon ground cinnamon
2 cups graham stick cookies
½ cup cinnamon-flavor pieces or semisweet chocolate pieces

WHAT YOU DO

1. Pop popcorn according to package directions. Open bag carefully and pour popcorn into a large bowl; remove all unpopped kernels.
2. In a small bowl combine sugar and cinnamon. Sprinkle cinnamon-sugar mixture over warm popcorn; toss until evenly coated. Add graham sticks. Let cool for 5 minutes. Toss in cinnamon chips. Makes 10 to 12 cups.

To Store: Place snack mix in an airtight container; cover. Store at room temperature for up to 1 week.

Tin Tower

Whether giving individual servings or enough for a family, stacked tins in any size make sturdy containers for delicious snack mix. Line each tin with a square of food-appropriate decorative tissue. Stack filled tins and secure in place with wide ribbons, knotting at the top. Slip contrasting ribbon under the knot and tie into a bow. Thread crafts wire through a large jingle bell and secure onto the bow. Repeat with a second jingle bell.

SNICKERDOODLE SNACK MIX

STAR MINT MERINGUES

Star Mint Meringues

WHAT YOU NEED

3 egg whites
¼ teaspoon cream of tartar
¼ teaspoon peppermint extract
⅛ teaspoon salt
¾ cup sugar
   Red paste food coloring

WHAT YOU DO

1. Preheat oven to 200°F. Line a cookie sheet with parchment paper; set aside. In a large mixing bowl combine egg whites, cream of tartar, peppermint extract, and salt. Beat with an electric mixer on medium until soft peaks form (tips curl). Gradually add sugar, about 1 tablespoon at a time, beating on high until stiff peaks form (tips stand straight).
2. With a clean small paintbrush, brush stripes of red paste food coloring on the inside of a pastry bag fitted with a ½-inch open star tip. Carefully transfer meringue into the bag. Pipe 2-inch stars 1 inch apart onto prepared cookie sheet.
3. Bake for 1½ hours or until meringues appear dry and are firm when lightly touched. Transfer cookies to a wire rack; let cool. Makes 24 cookies.
To Store: Layer cookies between sheets of waxed paper in an airtight container; cover. Store at room temperature for up to 3 days or freeze for up to 3 months.

Spiral Cherry Lollies

WHAT YOU NEED

¾ cup butter, softened
1 cup sugar
½ teaspoon baking powder
1 egg
1 teaspoon cherry extract
2 cups all-purpose flour
½ cup finely chopped red candied
   cherries
   Red paste food coloring
½ cup finely chopped green candied
   cherries
   Green paste food coloring
   Round paper lollipop sticks
¼ cup red and/or green nonpareils or
   sprinkles

WHAT YOU DO

1. In a large mixing bowl beat butter with an electric mixer on medium to high for 30 seconds. Add sugar and baking powder. Beat until combined, scraping sides of bowl occasionally. Beat in egg and cherry extract until combined. Beat in as much of the flour as you can with the mixer. Stir in any remaining flour. Divide dough in half. Stir red cherries into one dough portion; tint

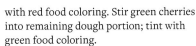

Jolly Lolly Vase

Cookies on a stick stand up straight when "potted" in a jar filled with heavy glass marbles. Tie velvet ribbon around the jar, knotting the ends. Tuck in a holiday pick near the knot.

SPIRAL CHERRY LOLLIES

with red food coloring. Stir green cherries into remaining dough portion; tint with green food coloring.
2. Divide each portion in half. Cover and chill dough about 1 hour or until easy to handle.
3. Between two pieces of waxed paper, roll one red dough portion into a 10×5-inch rectangle. Between two pieces of waxed paper, roll one green dough portion into a 10×5-inch rectangle. Remove the top layer of waxed paper from each rectangle. Invert the green rectangle on top of the red rectangle; remove top layer of waxed paper. Starting from a long side, roll up dough. Pinch dough edges to seal. Roll in half of the nonpareils and wrap in plastic wrap. Repeat with remaining dough portions and

nonpareils. Chill dough rolls for 1 to 2 hours or until very firm.
4. Preheat oven to 375°F. Lightly grease cookie sheets; set aside. Unwrap dough rolls; reshape, if necessary. Cut dough rolls crosswise into ½-inch-thick slices. Place slices 2 inches apart on the prepared cookie sheets. Push a craft stick into each slice, pressing dough around stick.
5. Bake about 10 minutes or until edges are firm and tops are set. Cool on cookie sheets for 1 minute. Transfer cookies to a wire rack and let cool. Makes 36 to 38 cookies.
To Store: Place cookies between sheets of waxed paper in an airtight container; cover. Store at room temperature for up to 3 days or freeze for up to 3 months.

In-a-Twinkling
brilliant bags

◄ Snowy Delight

Freehand snowflakes in marking pen lend casual flair to a plain white gift bag. Dot each flake with a brad poked through the center. Fold over the top of the gift bag, punch two holes, and tie on a large decorative snowflake with ribbon.

Tailor Made▼

Though there's no sewing required, this gift bag looks like it was sewn by a pro. Trace around a salad plate on the bag top; trim with scissors. Make a crease for flap. Hot-glue a trio of ribbon trims on one side of bag from bottom to crease. Hot-glue piping to wrong side of flap. Hot-glue piping around a button and adhere to bag front

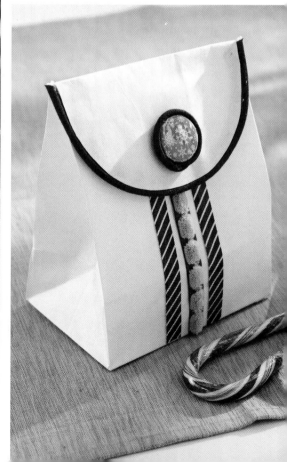

◄ Sticker Fun

Even kids will love decorating these bags! Start with a curved piece of glittered paper glued to the bag as a base. Then build a Christmas scene with dimensional stickers, using as many or few as you like.

Short and Sweet▼

Using decorative-edge scissors, cut off a paper bag to make it box shape. Snip down 1 inch on each corner using straight scissors. Make evenly spaced holes through the flap and the bag using a paper punch. Hot-glue a ribbon bow to the flap and press a holiday sticker on the front.

Jingle All the Way▶

Make a cardboard initial more festive by hot-gluing on tiny jingle bells. Fold over the top of the bag and trim with a folded paper doily. Punch two small holes through the bag and flap, one under the other. Use a decorative pick to hold the flap closed.

kids

Inspire little ones to share their enthusiasm of the season by making lovingly crafted trims.

Marching Men

Penguins have a cute way about them, and these characters are spot-on adorable.

Gang's All Here

Once plain wooden eggs, these penguins have personality plus with their painted features and simple trim details.

WHAT YOU NEED

2½-inch-tall wooden egg
Acrylic paint in black, white, and medium orange
Paintbrush
Cotton swab
Black paper
Scissors
Hot-glue gun and glue sticks
Trims, such as pom-poms and chenille stems

WHAT YOU DO

1. On a covered work area, paint egg black. Let paint dry.
2. Using the photo as a guide, paint a half circle on the bottom portion of the egg for the belly. Using a tiny brush, spread out the paint along the outer edge to look wispy. Paint a U shape for the face, rounding the top points for the eye area. Let the white paint dry.
3. Paint a tiny orange beak inside the U shape. Dip the cotton swab in black paint and dot eyes; let dry.
4. For wings, fold a 2-inch square of black paper in half. Cut out a teardrop shape. With points down, hot-glue a wing to each side of penguin. The glue gun is hot, so ask for an adult's help if needed.
5. Shape a hat, scarf, or earmuffs from chenille stem; hot-glue in place. Add pom-pom accents where desired.

Polka-Dot Pair

Whether hanging from Christmas tree branches or perched on packages, these painted fellows are sure to bring smiles.

WHAT YOU NEED

(all pieces can be wood or medium-weight cardboard shapes)
Paintbrushes
Acrylic paints in black, white, orange, and other desired colors
4-inch-high oval
Two 1½-inch-long teardrops
1¾-inch-diameter circle
Triangle, 1½ inches on long edge
Triangle, ¾ inches on long edge
2-inch-long craft stick
Small flower shape
Toothpick
Cotton swab
4-inch length of string

WHAT YOU DO

1. On a covered work area, paint oval and teardrop shapes black. Paint circle white. Paint small triangle orange. Let paint dry.
2. Paint remaining pieces a solid color as desired for hat. Let paint dry.
3. To make large polka dots on wings, dip cotton swab into white paint and dot onto teardrop shapes. Repeat until wings are covered, leaving black space between painted dots. To make rings of small dots, dip a toothpick into paint and dot onto teardrop shapes. Continue dotting in ring patterns until teardrop shapes are covered. Let paint dry.
4. Paint stripes, plaid, or dots onto hat pieces; let dry.
5. Using the photo as a guide, hot-glue the white belly piece on the black oval. Glue the wings, beak, and hat pieces in place. The glue gun is hot, so ask for an adult's help if needed.
6. Dip the end of a paintbrush into white paint and dot onto oval as shown in photo. Let paint dry. Dip the end of a toothpick in black paint and dot in the center of each white dot; let dry.
7. Hot-glue a loop of string on the back of the penguin for hanging.

Jolly Potato Prints

Just like snowflakes, these guys and gals of the snow variety are all unique and special.

Happy Holidays Card

Wish family and friends "Merry Christmas" by sending a trio of smiles their way.

WHAT YOU NEED

5×8-inch piece of light blue snowflake paper
5¼×8¼-inch piece of white paper
11½×8¾-inch piece of purple paper, folded with short ends together
Potatoes
Knife
Paper plate
Acrylic paint in light blue, white, black, and other desired colors
Glue stick
Toothpick

WHAT YOU DO

1. On a cutting board and using a knife, carefully cut two potatoes, one larger flat side for snowman body, one smaller flat side for head as shown in Photo A. The knife is sharp, so ask for an adult's help if needed.
2. Squeeze some light blue paint onto a paper plate. Dip potato cut for snowman's body into blue paint and press onto snowflake paper as shown in Photo B. Let paint dry. Wash off paint from potato. Repeat with white paint, moving potato to right a little to create the look of a shadow. Let the paint dry.

3. Cut a top hat shape from potato to fit head shape. Dip into blue paint and press onto snowman heads as shown in Photo C.
4. Use glue stick to adhere card top to white paper, then to purple paper.
5. Using the photo for ideas, cut potato shapes into strips or half ovals to make scarves. Stamp scarves with blue first, let dry, then follow with another color; let dry. Add hat bands. Let dry.
6. To make arms, use short pieces of thin cardboard. Dip edge into black paint and press onto card as shown in Photo D. To make "fingers," fold cardboard into a V shape, dip into paint, and press near end of arm print. Let the paint dry.
7. Make buttons by dipping a pencil eraser into paint and dotting onto snowman. Dot with blue first, let dry, then use a color as shown in Photo E. Let dry.
8. To make eyes, dip handle end of a paintbrush into light blue paint; dot onto snowman face. Let paint dry. Dot eyes with black using a toothpick dipped into paint. Cut a triangle from potato, dip into light blue paint, and dot on face. Rinse off potato. Stamp nose with orange paint.
9. Use a toothpick to dot on smiles.

Surprise Sleeves

Library card sleeves, available at school supply stores, transform into merry gift envelopes when stamped with one-of-a-kind potato-print snowmen. Use the techniques learned on the greeting card, pages 142–143, to create the designs.

Snow-Loving Sir

Create a wintry work of art to frame and display with pride.

WHAT YOU NEED

4½×6½-inch piece of blue cardstock
5×7-inch piece of white cardstock
Glue stick
Potato
Knife
Paper plate
Acrylic paint in white, purple, black, orange, and other desired colors
Glue stick
Toothpick
2-inch square of thin cardboard
Straws in large and small sizes
Fine paintbrush, optional
Frame

WHAT YOU DO

1. Using glue stick, adhere blue paper on top of white paper.
2. On a cutting board and using a knife, carefully cut a potato in half. The knife is sharp, so ask for an adult's help if needed.
3. Squeeze some white paint onto plate. Dip cut side of potato into paint and dab onto bottom of blue paper to make the snow. Repeat as needed to make a mounded row. Rinse off paint from potato if it starts to dry.
4. Put more white paint on plate if needed. Squeeze a small amount of purple paint onto plate. Dip potato into white paint, then roll potato edge in purple paint. Press potato onto blue paper using the photo as a guide for placement. Let paint dry. Wash off paint from potato. Repeat with white paint only for the head. Let the paint dry.
5. Cut top hat, carrot nose, and scarf shapes from potato. Potato-print the snowman using orange paint for the nose and desired colors for the hat and scarf. Let the paint dry.
6. Cut a short piece of cardboard for arms. Dip end into black paint and press onto snowman body. Repeat for the "fingers," using shorter pieces of cardboard. Let the paint dry. Use this same technique for making scarf fringes.
7. To make a tree, fold cardboard in half. Hold V shape with point at top. Dip end of cardboard into green paint. Dot onto paper several times, starting at ground and moving upward until tree height is reached as shown in Photo A. Get more paint on the cardboard as needed. Dip the eraser end of a pencil into yellow paint to dot a "star" at the top of the tree. Let the paint dry.
8. To make snowflakes, dip end of small straw in white paint and press onto the blue sky. Repeat with the large straw as shown in Photo B. Let the paint dry.
9. To make eyes, dip the handle end of a paintbrush into black paint; dot onto snowman face. Let paint dry. Dot the smile using a toothpick dipped into black paint as shown in Photo C. Let paint dry.
10. Insert the painting into the frame.

Branch Brighteners

A little paint, a little glitter, and bright holiday ornaments become family favorites.

Welcome Home

Paint a tiny scene and dust it with glitter to create a mini wintry wonderland.

WHAT YOU NEED

Christmas ornaments in bright muted
  colors
Acrylic metallic paint in white and colors
  to coordinate with ornament
Paintbrush
Fine white glitter

WHAT YOU DO

1. Paint a rectangle for house, making the roofline pointed as shown in Photo A. Paint a second house in another color if desired. Let the paint dry.
2. Use white paint to paint roof lines and windows as shown in Photo B. Let the paint dry.
3. Paint a simple tree as shown in Photo C; let dry.
4. Paint the snowy ground as shown in Photo D. Use a toothpick dipped in white paint to dot the sky with snowflakes as shown in Photo E. Let the paint dry.
5. Paint a second coat of white on the ground area and on roofline and sprinkle with glitter as shown in Photo F; let dry.

Texture Time

The secret to these cool ornaments is a fan brush, metallic paint, and a super-simple painting technique.

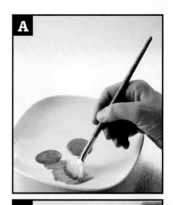

WHAT YOU NEED

Acrylic metallic paint in a variety
  of colors
Fan paintbrush
Plate
Christmas ornaments in muted colors

WHAT YOU DO

1. Dip paintbrush in paint. Brush back and forth on plate to remove some of paint as shown in Photo A.

2. Brush paint onto ornament in one direction as shown in Photo B. Load brush again with paint as in Step 1; brush paint in opposite direction, making an X as shown in Photo C. Use the same color on the entire ornament or blend in new colors as desired. Let the paint dry.

In-A-Twinkling
paper play

◀ Top It Off

Decorative paper strips make pretty bows. Consider the package size, then decide how wide to make the strips. Start with 12-inch lengths, cutting shorter if needed for desired bow size. Tape ends together. Overlap the three rings and staple in the center. Hot-glue the bow to the package along with jingle bells. The gun is hot, so ask for help if needed.

Pretty Plate ▼

Give a square paper plate a holiday face-lift. Place stickers on one corner. Use a ruler to mark the edge every ½ inch. Punch holes where marked, avoiding sticker areas. Cut thin paper strips to thread through holes, taping ends on the back. Use a 1-inch circle maker to cut circles from papers. Tape a strip together, then tape to back of plate.

Canned Goods

Peanut cans, washed and dried, recycle into gift containers. Cut a strip of paper to wrap the can and tape at the seam. Find a jar or can slightly smaller than the lid and trace around it on print paper; cut out. Adhere the circle to the lid using double-sided tape. Poke a hole in the center of the lid with an ice pick. Ask an adult to help if needed. Thread a jingle bell onto half a chenille stem; twist to secure, leaving ½-inch tails. Thread tails through hole in lid and spread tails apart to hold "handle" in place. Trim front of can with a sticker.

Frilly Frame

Package toppers, ornaments, fridge magnets! To make one, use a glue stick to attach a mini holiday-print cupcake liner over a traditional one. Cut a photo into a circle; glue in place. Shape chenille stems to edge photo and hot-glue around photo.

Tag Cuties ▲

Get ready to win the best tag award! Trace patterns on page 155; cut out. Use patterns to cut face, nose, and hat. Use decorative-edge scissors to cut brims. Using pattern markings as guides, punch out eyes and smile using a ⅛-inch paper punch. Back the shape with black paper; trim with pinking shears. Adhere pieces with glue stick. Punch a hole at the top for hanging.

patterns

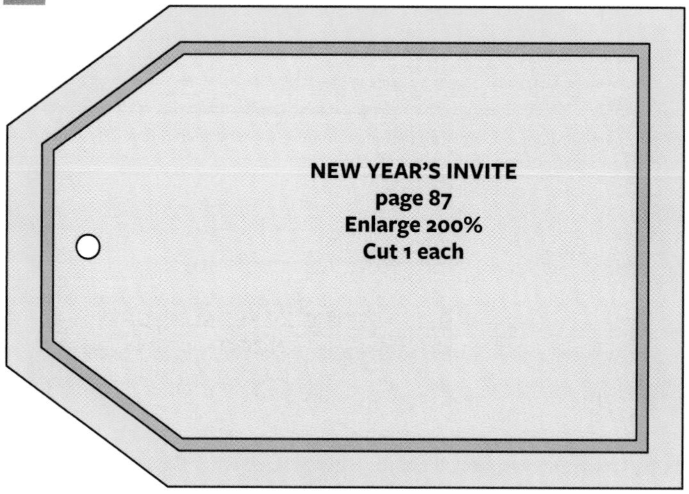

NEW YEAR'S INVITE
page 87
Enlarge 200%
Cut 1 each

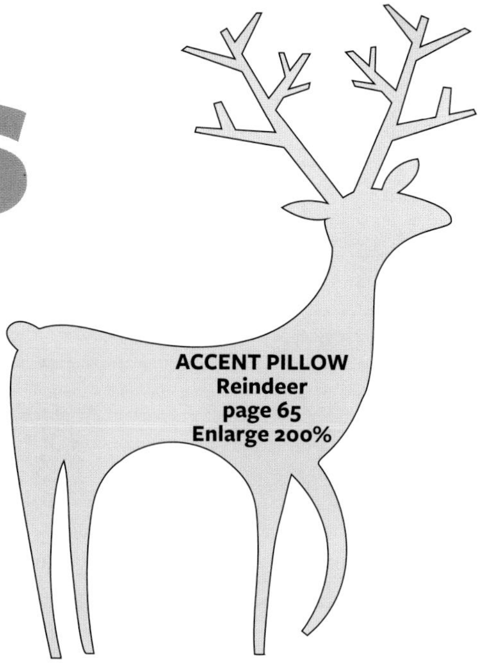

ACCENT PILLOW
Reindeer
page 65
Enlarge 200%

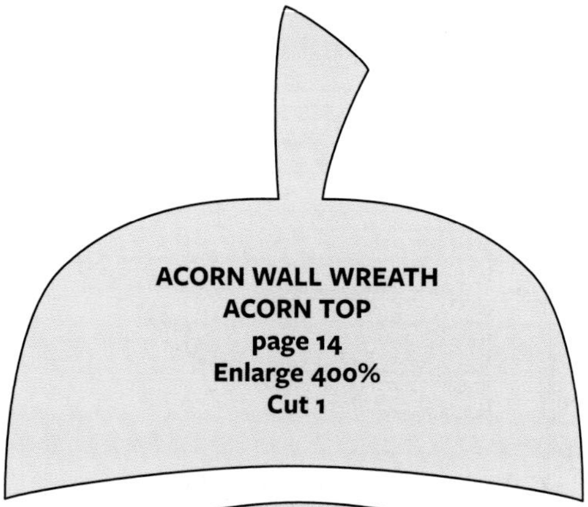

ACORN WALL WREATH
ACORN TOP
page 14
Enlarge 400%
Cut 1

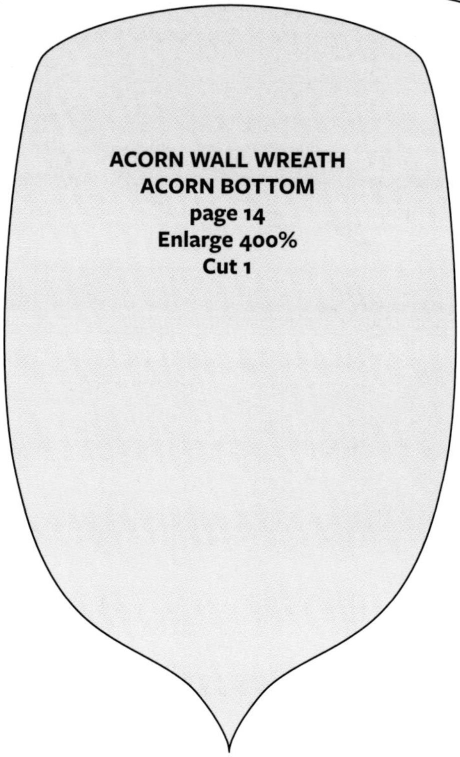

ACORN WALL WREATH
ACORN BOTTOM
page 14
Enlarge 400%
Cut 1

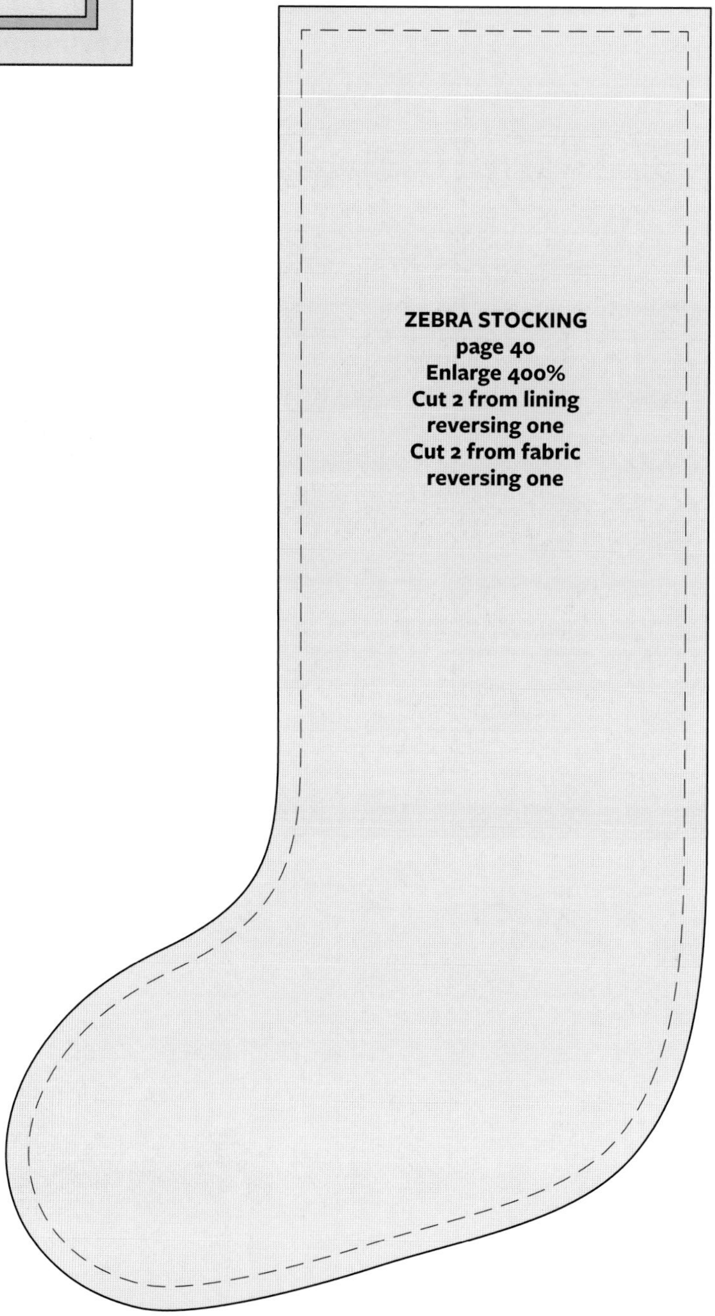

ZEBRA STOCKING
page 40
Enlarge 400%
Cut 2 from lining
reversing one
Cut 2 from fabric
reversing one

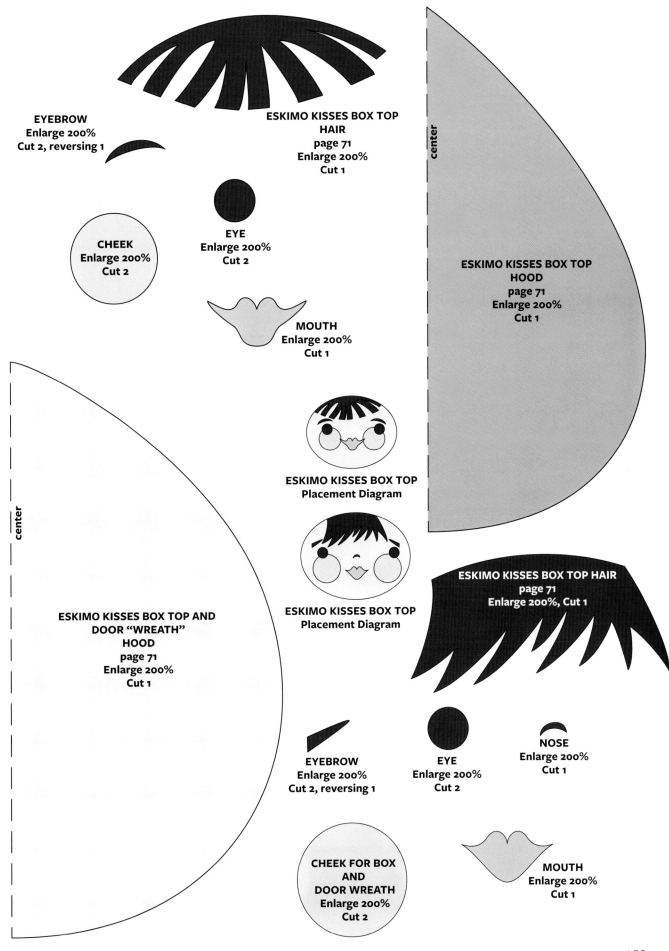

EYEBROW
Enlarge 200%
Cut 2, reversing 1

ESKIMO KISSES BOX TOP HAIR
page 71
Enlarge 200%
Cut 1

center

EYE
Enlarge 200%
Cut 2

CHEEK
Enlarge 200%
Cut 2

ESKIMO KISSES BOX TOP HOOD
page 71
Enlarge 200%
Cut 1

MOUTH
Enlarge 200%
Cut 1

ESKIMO KISSES BOX TOP
Placement Diagram

ESKIMO KISSES BOX TOP
Placement Diagram

center

ESKIMO KISSES BOX TOP AND DOOR "WREATH" HOOD
page 71
Enlarge 200%
Cut 1

ESKIMO KISSES BOX TOP HAIR
page 71
Enlarge 200%, Cut 1

EYEBROW
Enlarge 200%
Cut 2, reversing 1

EYE
Enlarge 200%
Cut 2

NOSE
Enlarge 200%
Cut 1

CHEEK FOR BOX AND DOOR WREATH
Enlarge 200%
Cut 2

MOUTH
Enlarge 200%
Cut 1

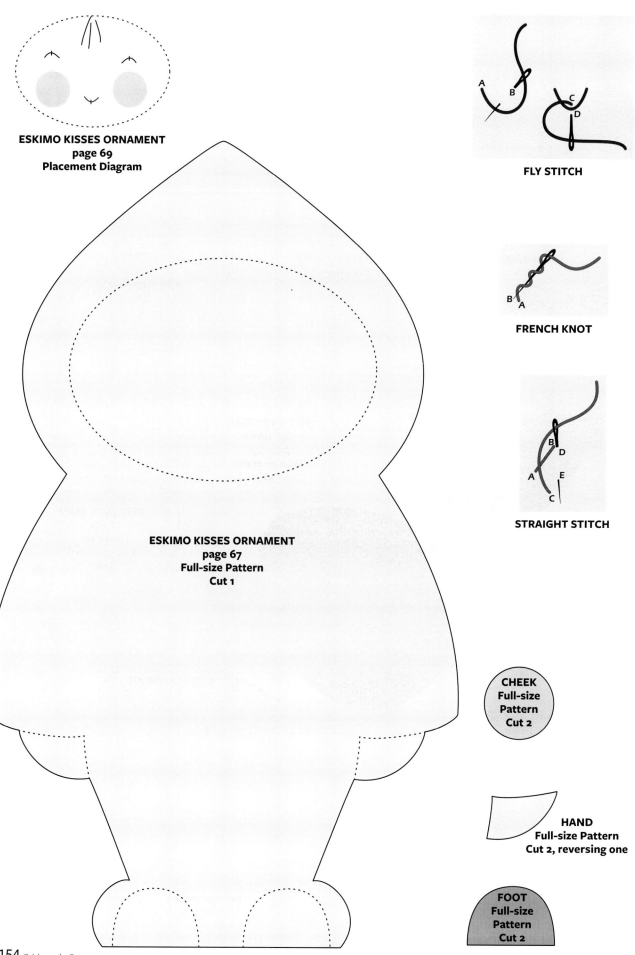

ESKIMO KISSES ORNAMENT
page 69
Placement Diagram

FLY STITCH

FRENCH KNOT

STRAIGHT STITCH

ESKIMO KISSES ORNAMENT
page 67
Full-size Pattern
Cut 1

CHEEK
Full-size
Pattern
Cut 2

HAND
Full-size Pattern
Cut 2, reversing one

FOOT
Full-size
Pattern
Cut 2

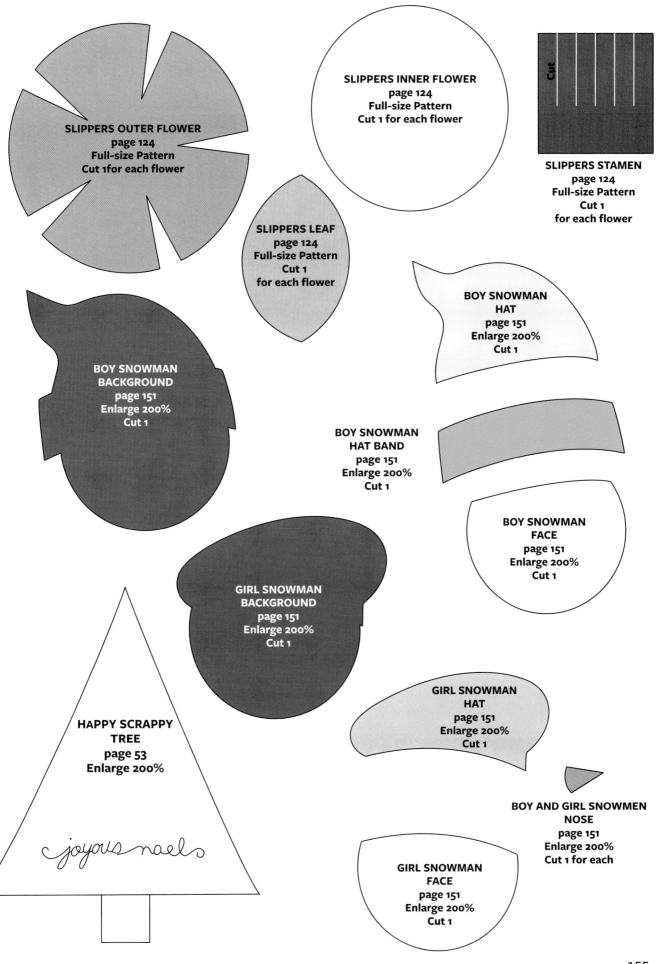

SLIPPERS OUTER FLOWER
page 124
Full-size Pattern
Cut 1for each flower

SLIPPERS INNER FLOWER
page 124
Full-size Pattern
Cut 1 for each flower

Cut

SLIPPERS STAMEN
page 124
Full-size Pattern
Cut 1
for each flower

SLIPPERS LEAF
page 124
Full-size Pattern
Cut 1
for each flower

BOY SNOWMAN
HAT
page 151
Enlarge 200%
Cut 1

BOY SNOWMAN
BACKGROUND
page 151
Enlarge 200%
Cut 1

BOY SNOWMAN
HAT BAND
page 151
Enlarge 200%
Cut 1

BOY SNOWMAN
FACE
page 151
Enlarge 200%
Cut 1

GIRL SNOWMAN
BACKGROUND
page 151
Enlarge 200%
Cut 1

GIRL SNOWMAN
HAT
page 151
Enlarge 200%
Cut 1

HAPPY SCRAPPY
TREE
page 53
Enlarge 200%

joyous naels

BOY AND GIRL SNOWMEN
NOSE
page 151
Enlarge 200%
Cut 1 for each

GIRL SNOWMAN
FACE
page 151
Enlarge 200%
Cut 1

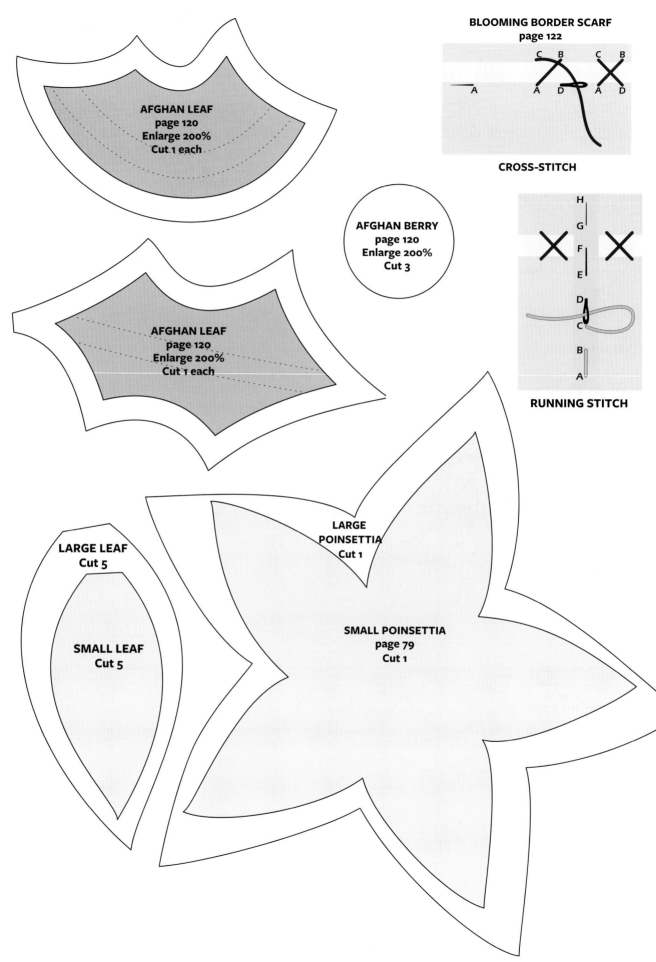

AFGHAN LEAF
page 120
Enlarge 200%
Cut 1 each

AFGHAN BERRY
page 120
Enlarge 200%
Cut 3

AFGHAN LEAF
page 120
Enlarge 200%
Cut 1 each

BLOOMING BORDER SCARF
page 122

C B   C B

A   A D   A D

CROSS-STITCH

H
G
F
E

D
C

B

A

RUNNING STITCH

LARGE LEAF
Cut 5

SMALL LEAF
Cut 5

LARGE POINSETTIA
Cut 1

SMALL POINSETTIA
page 79
Cut 1

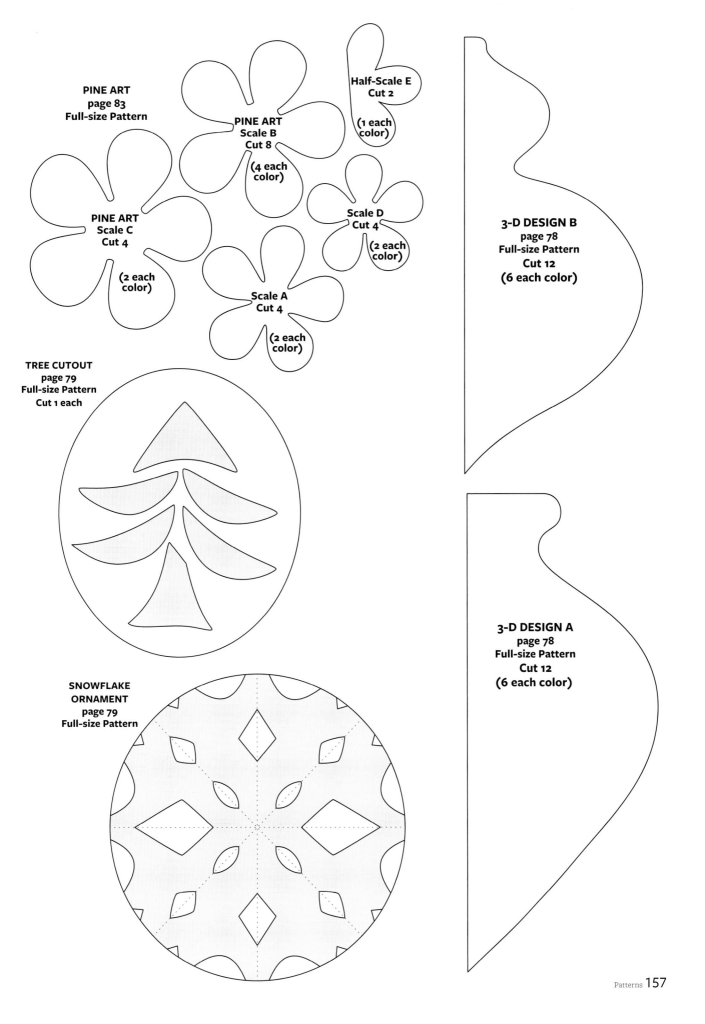

PINE ART
page 83
Full-size Pattern

PINE ART
Scale B
Cut 8
(4 each color)

Half-Scale E
Cut 2
(1 each color)

PINE ART
Scale C
Cut 4
(2 each color)

Scale D
Cut 4
(2 each color)

Scale A
Cut 4
(2 each color)

3-D DESIGN B
page 78
Full-size Pattern
Cut 12
(6 each color)

TREE CUTOUT
page 79
Full-size Pattern
Cut 1 each

3-D DESIGN A
page 78
Full-size Pattern
Cut 12
(6 each color)

SNOWFLAKE
ORNAMENT
page 79
Full-size Pattern

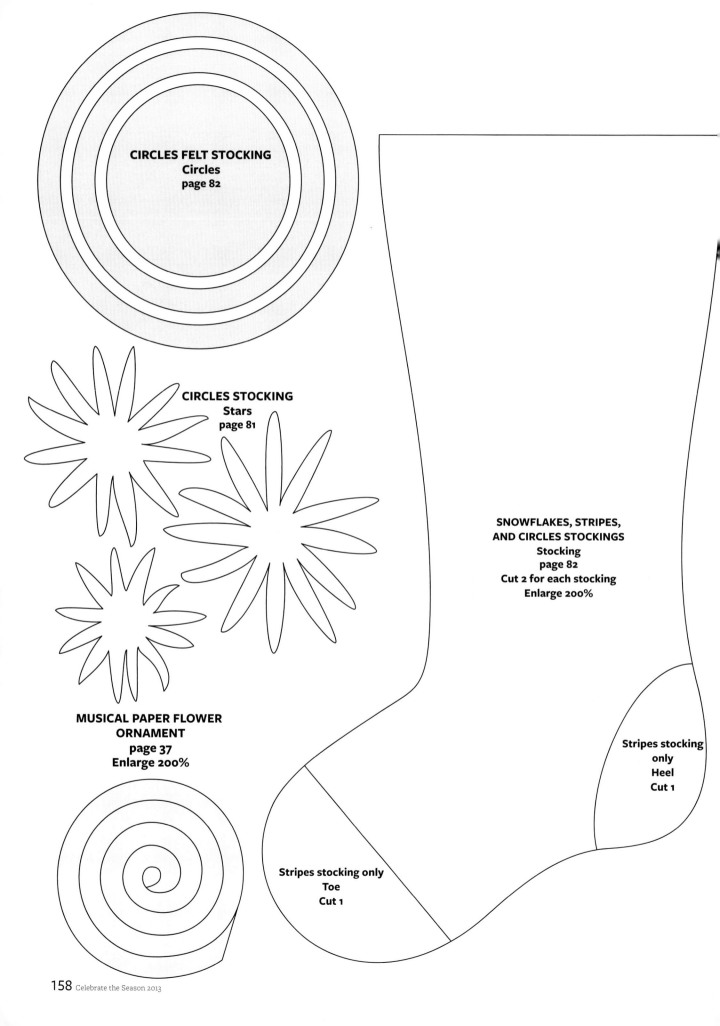

CIRCLES FELT STOCKING
Circles
page 82

CIRCLES STOCKING
Stars
page 81

SNOWFLAKES, STRIPES, AND CIRCLES STOCKINGS
Stocking
page 82
Cut 2 for each stocking
Enlarge 200%

Stripes stocking only
Heel
Cut 1

MUSICAL PAPER FLOWER ORNAMENT
page 37
Enlarge 200%

Stripes stocking only
Toe
Cut 1

index

index *continued*

CREDITS

FOOD STYLISTS
Jennifer Peterson
Charles Worthington

PHOTO STYLING
Sue Banker and
Cathy Brett

PHOTOGRAPHY
Jay Wilde
Marty Baldwin
Jason Donnelly

PROJECT DESIGNS
Sue Banker